Christmas

The Annual of Christmas Literature and Art

FROM **The Messiah**

Luke 2:10,11

George Frederich Handel

And the an-gel said un-to them, Fear not

for be-hold, I bring you good ti-dings of great

Joy, which shall be to all peo-ple. For

un-to you is born this day in the cit-y of

David a Sav-ior, which is Christ the Lord.

Christmas

The Annual of Christmas Literature and Art

FOUNDED BY RANDOLPH E. HAUGAN, EDITOR VOLUMES ONE THROUGH FIFTY

Volume Fifty-five

Augsburg Publishing House
Minneapolis, Minnesota

Randolph Edgar Haugan

July 31, 1902–February 18, 1985

On February 18, 1985, Randolph Haugan, who lived in wonder and awe of the Bethlehem-born king, joined that heavenly throng whose message of "Glory to God in the highest" he published for 50 years.

At the age of 26 Haugan was named general manager of the fledgling Augsburg Publishing House. For 41 years he built an organization which now ranks with the leading religious publishing institutions of this century. During those demanding years his interest in the Christmas gospel grew into one of his major passions. He collected art, sculpture, a vast library of Christmas literature, and artifacts which present or interpret the Savior's birth. He became an authority on the American phenomenon in which the ethnic customs and traditions of immigrants are perpetuated through family celebrations of God's great gift.

Out of his vast Christmas knowledge he created *CHRISTMAS: The Annual of Christmas Literature and Art.* For 50 years he edited his "Christmas Annual," creating an American tradition for thousands and thousands of families.

This 55th volume of *CHRISTMAS* is dedicated to the memory of Randolph Haugan, whose life and work helped those who knew him and those who read the annual focus on the Christ child—God's "with-you" gift to all humankind.

May your celebration of God's gift-giving event be richer because of this and subsequent volumes created in the tradition begun by Randolph Haugan.

Table of Contents

Editorial staff: Leonard Flachman, Karen Walhof, Jennifer Fast; Richard Hillert, music consultant

Copyright © 1985 Augsburg Publishing House
All rights reserved. Manufactured in the United States of America
Library of Congress Catalog Card No. 32-30914
International Standard Book No. 0-8066-8966-8 (paper) 0-8066-8967-6 (cloth)

The Christmas Story

According to St. Luke and St. Matthew

VIRGINIA BRODERICK

And it came to pass in those days that a decree went out from Caesar Augustus that all the world should be registered. This census first took place while Quirinius was governing Syria.

And all went to be registered, everyone to his own city.

And Joseph also went up from Galilee, out of the city of Nazareth, into Judea, to the city of David, which is called Bethlehem, because he was of the house and lineage of David, to be registered with Mary, his betrothed wife, who was with child.

And so it was, that while they were there, the days were completed that she should be delivered.

And she brought forth her firstborn son, and wrapped him in swaddling cloths, and laid him in a manger, because there was no room for them in the inn.

And there were in the same country shepherds living out in the fields, keeping watch over their flock by night.

And behold, an angel of the Lord stood before them, and the glory of the Lord shone around them, and they were greatly afraid.

VIRGINIA BRODERICK

$\mathcal{A}$nd the angel said to them, "Do not be afraid, for behold, I bring you good tidings of great joy which will be to all people. For there is born to you this day in the city of David a Savior, who is Christ the Lord.

"And this will be a sign to you: You will find a babe wrapped in swaddling cloths, lying in a manger."

And suddenly there was with the angel a multitude of the heavenly host praising God and saying: "Glory to God in the highest, and on earth peace, good will toward men!"

And so it was, when the angels had gone away from them into heaven, that the shepherds said to one another, "Let us now go to Bethlehem and see this thing that has come to pass, which the Lord has made known to us."

And they came with haste and found Mary and Joseph, and the babe lying in a manger.

And when they had seen it, they made widely known the saying which was told them concerning this child.

And all those who heard it marveled at those things which were told them by the shepherds.

But Mary kept all these things and pondered them in her heart.

And the shepherds returned, glorifying and praising God for all the things that they had heard and seen, as it was told to them.

N ow after Jesus was born in Bethlehem of Judea in the days of Herod the king, behold, wise men from the East came to Jerusalem, saying, 'Where is he who has been born King of the Jews? For we have seen his star in the East and have come to worship him.''

When Herod the king had heard these things, he was troubled, and all Jerusalem with him.

And when he had gathered all the chief priests and scribes of the people together, he inquired of them where the Christ was to be born.

And they said to him, "In Bethlehem of Judea, for thus it is written by the prophet:

'And you, Bethlehem, in the land of Judah,
Are not the least among the rulers of Judah;
For out of you will come a Ruler
Who will shepherd my people Israel.' "

Then Herod, when he had secretly called the wise men, determined from them what time the star appeared.

And he sent them to Bethlehem and said, "Go and search diligently for the young child, and when you have found him, bring back word to me, that I may come and worship him also."

When they had heard the king, they departed; and behold, the star which they had seen in the East went before them, till it came and stood over where the young child was.

When they saw the star, they rejoiced with exceedingly great joy.

And when they had come into the house, they saw the young child with Mary his mother, and fell down and worshiped him. And when they had opened their treasures, they presented gifts to him: gold, frankincense, and myrrh.

And being warned by God in a dream that they should not return to Herod, they departed for their own country another way.

VIRGINIA BRODERICK

*A*nd when they had departed, behold, an angel of the Lord appeared to Joseph in a dream, saying, "Arise, take the young child and his mother, flee to Egypt, and stay there until I bring you word; for Herod will seek the young child to destroy him."

When he arose, he took the young child and his mother by night and departed into Egypt, and was there until the death of Herod, that it might be fulfilled which was spoken by the Lord through the prophet, saying, "Out of Egypt I have called my son."

But when Herod was dead, behold, an angel of the Lord appeared in a dream to Joseph in Egypt, saying, "Arise, take the young child and his mother, and go into the land of Israel, for those who sought the young child's life are dead."

And he arose, took the young child and his mother, and came into the land of Israel.

12

A Carol in Prose

W. A. POOVEY

It is full of the tang of snow and cold air and crisp green holly leaves, and warm with the glow of crimson holly berries, blazing hearths and human hearts." So Edgar Johnson described Charles Dickens' *A Christmas Carol.* But, however eloquent, no single sentence can do justice to the story of Ebenezer Scrooge and his encounter with ghosts one Christmas Eve.

Dickens worked more than a month on the story, walking the dark, unlit streets of London at night, weeping and laughing and weeping again as he planned the plot and created the characters. When it was published, Dickens wrote to a friend: "The *Carol* is the greatest success, I am told, that this ruffian and rascal has ever achieved."

A Christmas Carol proved an overnight success, selling 6000 copies the first day it was published. Second and third printings were authorized the very next day. Dickens' contemporaries recognized *A Christmas Carol* as a masterpiece almost immediately. William Thackery, a famous writer of that era, said, "It seems to me a national benefit, and to every man or woman who reads it a personal kindness."

The tale of Ebenezer Scrooge has never lost that first popularity. *A Christmas Carol* has been rewritten as a musical, transformed into an opera, and produced both live and in animation for television. The location of the story has been shifted from London to New England and even to the desert land of Arizona, but the plot remains the same: an old miser is moved to change his ways after a visitation by three ghosts.

Scrooge's Third Visitor by John Leech from the first edition.

For a time Charles Dickens made a career of reading the *Carol* to audiences on both sides of the Atlantic. As an indication of the continuing popularity of this carol in prose, the original manuscript, showing countless corrections made by the author, is now in the Pierpont Morgan Library in New York City and is the most asked for item among that library's treasures.

Charles Dickens, however, did not start out to create a masterpiece. He wrote the story in order to earn some money. Although by 1843 Dickens had become a successful and widely acclaimed novelist, his financial needs were great. He had the care of a growing family plus a number of relatives who looked to him for support. One of these was his father, the model for Mr. Micawber in *David Copperfield* who was always hoping something would turn up to help him out of his difficulties. Dickens conceived the idea of publishing a Christmas story; the sale of which would help relieve his financial problems. Unfortunately, due to poor planning, the *Carol* did not make as much profit as the author had hoped. Yet the whole world remains in Dickens' debt. Countless readers have thrilled to the lines: "Marley was dead: to begin with. There is no doubt whatever about that . . . ."

But what gives this famous story such lasting appeal? Part of the story's appeal lies in the sly humor, the exaggeration, that is characteristic of Dickens' writings. Scrooge is declared to be so cold that "he carried his own low temperature always about with him; he iced his office in the dog-days; and didn't thaw it one degree at Christmas." Dickens also relates that blind men's dogs tugged their owners out of the way of Scrooge as if to say, "No eye at all is better than an evil eye, dark master!"

We are amused by the description of other characters as well. Mrs. Fezziwig is described as "one vast substantial smile." The fiddler at the Fezziwig ball plunges his face into a pot of porter, only to begin again as if he were a new fiddler and the other one was carried home, exhausted, on a shutter. The children in the house where Scrooge's former sweetheart lived are described not as forty behaving as one but as every child behaving like forty. We have all known children like that.

Even the inanimate objects in the story are dealt with playfully. The house where Scrooge lives is said to have played hide-and-seek with other houses when young and to have lost its way out and so grown old in the midst of office buildings. Dickens declares Marley "dead as a door-nail" and then observes that a coffin-nail would seem to be the deadest piece of hardware. But he refuses to disturb the hallowed simile of a door-nail and so repeats his original statement.

Yet even more endearing and enduring than his humor is the long slate of characters Dickens has given the world: Pickwick, David Copperfield, Fagin, Bill Sykes, Little Nell, Mr. Micawber, and a host of others. Some have insisted his characters are more like caricatures than finished portraits. Be that as it may, readers still respond warmly to Dickens' cast.

Likewise, *A Christmas Carol* introduces its share of memorable characters. Some of their names have even become part of our language. Take, for example, Ebenezer Scrooge. Can you think of a better name for a miser? We use his name to describe a tight-fisted individual: "He was a regular scrooge," we say. But Dickens puts it best when he introduces Scrooge to his readers:

Oh! But he was a tight-fisted hand at the grindstone, Scrooge! a squeezing, wrenching, grasping, scraping, clutching, coveteous old sinner! Hard and sharp as flint, from which no steel had ever struck out generous fire; secret, and self-contained, and solitary as an oyster.

It is hard not to dislike the man from the beginning. He starves and freezes his office clerk; he swears at his nephew who has simply stopped by to wish him a Merry Christmas; he refuses to make any charitable contributions to the poor; he even frightens off a small boy who tries to sing a Christmas carol at the keyhole. Scrooge is a despicable man.

And yet as the story unfolds we do not come to hope Scrooge will "get his," but that he will change for the better. Dickens cleverly shows us the youthful Ebenezer deserted by everyone and left to spend Christmas at a boarding school. We also see what Scrooge sacrifices in his pursuit of money—the girl he once loved, a pleasant dinner with his nephew, and the warmth of human contact. So when the Ghost of Christmas Yet to Come reveals that Scrooge is destined to die in a bare bedroom with no one to mourn his passing, we rejoice to witness a repentant Scrooge and open our hearts to the changed man.

Tiny Tim is probably the second most popular character in the story. The crippled son of Scrooge's clerk, Bob Cratchit, Tiny Tim will die unless help comes to the struggling Cratchit family. The dear little fellow accompanies his father to church on Christmas Day in the hope that those who see him will be reminded of the one who made lame beggars walk and blind men see. The lad ends the story with those cheery words: "God Bless Us Every One!"

Page one from Dickens' original handwritten manuscript, now housed in the Pierpont Morgan Library. It reads: "Marley was dead: to begin with. There is no doubt whatever about that. The register of his burial was signed by the clergyman, the clerk, the undertaker, and the chief mourner. Scrooge signed it: and Scrooge's name was good upon 'Change, for anything he chose to put his hand to. Old Marley was as dead as a door-nail.

"Mind! I don't mean to say that I know, of my own knowledge, what there is particularly dead about a door-nail. I might have been inclined, myself, to regard a coffin-nail as the deadest piece of ironmongery in the trade. But the wisdom of our ancestors is in the simile; and my unhallowed hands shall not disturb it, or the Country's done for. You will therefore permit me to repeat, emphatically, that Marley was as dead as a door-nail.

"Scrooge knew he was dead[...] course he did. How could [...] otherwise? Scrooge and he [...] partners for I don't kno[...] many years. Scrooge was [...] executor, his sole admin[...] his sole assign, his sole [...] legatee, his sole friend [...] mourner. And even S[...] not so dreadfully cut u[...] event, but that he was[...] man of business on [...] of the funeral, and [...] with an undoubted [...]

And on Dickens [...] a tale of humor, [...] or, to our contin[...]

Bob Cratchit, Scrooge's clerk, doesn't impress us *as a very strong character*. We wish he *would, just once, tell off his miserly employer*. Yet even at home and away from Scrooge, he still speaks gently about him. More to our liking is the bustling figure of Mrs. Cratchit as she prepares dinner for her numerous family. She worries about the goose and is almost too nervous to take out the pudding and bring it to the table. But when she enters, flushed and smiling proudly, her husband declares the pudding the greatest success achieved by Mrs. Cratchit since their marriage.

But when Bob Cratchit proposes a toast to "Mr. Scrooge, the Founder of the Feast," Mrs. Cratchit objects: "The Founder of the Feast indeed! I wish I had him here. I'd give him a piece of my mind to feast upon, and I hope he'd have a good appetite for it." We feel like standing up and cheering for Mrs. Cratchit and all the faithful wives who suffer when their husbands are mistreated by employers. Mrs Cratchit is a gem.

Other endearing characters include Peter Cratchit, Scrooge's nephew, the pretty niece, the amorous Topper, Old Fezziwig, the rascals who steal Scrooge's possessions, and the ghost of Old Marley. More than 30 separate individuals are described in this short story. It is no wonder the material can be dramatized so easily; it contains such colorful roles.

Yet characters alone, whether

Mr. Fezziwig's Ball by John Leech from the first edition.

Memories of a Christmas Carol

PHILLIP SNYDER

In the 1940s and early 1950s, when I was growing up, our family of five and an equal number of relatives would gather around the radio in the living room on Christmas Eve to hear Lionel Barrymore read the part of Scrooge Charles Dickens' *A Christmas Carol*. That time, not after supper and before we left for church, was the memorable part of a magical evening. My twin her and I delighted to miss our normal bedtime.

radio was a capacious wooden console with a short-band. Hours earlier, while decorating the Christ-ee, we had listened to King George VI's Christmas via the BBC. By the 1950s, if we were lucky tmospheric conditions were just right, we could prerecorded program from several successive Listening to Barrymore's hoarse, rasping ph and growl was a sublime, heart-warming rred in my memory only by the frustration gerly about a darkened Christmas tree in e burned-out bulb, which would inev-urse of the evening, put out the entire

ymore's famous *Carol* broadcasts had ive" from Hollywood to a rapturous on Christmas Day 1933. Over the nd sponsors went, but Barrymore's tradition. It would no doubt have ore to know the pleasure the s has given me, boy and man. lthough he had played many Ebenezer Scrooge he hoped that squeezing, wrenching, covetous old sinner, not e became—the converted

Scrooge who said humbly, "I will honour Christmas in my heart, and try to keep it all the year."

Lionel Barrymore was the Radio Age version of an old and fond Victorian custom now virtually lost, father's Christmas reading of Dickens' evocative ghost story. The Victorian family was never at a loss for things to do after dinner. There were games to play, songs to sing, recitations from the children (in Winchester, Virginia, in 1869 a boy learned 1,863 Bible verses during the year), and books to be read aloud.

Indeed, immediately upon the *Carol*'s publication in 1843, Dickens' friend John Foster wrote, "There poured upon (Dickens) daily, all through that Christmastime, letters from complete strangers to him, which I remember reading with a wonder of pleasure; not literary at all, but of the simplest domestic kind; of which the general burden was to tell him, amid many confidences, about their homes, how the *Carol* had come to be read aloud there and was to be kept upon a little shelf by itself, and was to do them no end of good."

On both sides of the Atlantic, the little book in its crimson and gold binding, with four illustrations by the Punch artist John Leech, appealed to rich and poor alike. Ultimately, the American financier John Pierpont Morgan bought Dickens' original manuscript. Old "J. P." used to have his librarian, Miss Belle da Costa Greene, read it to him every Christmas. And Scrooge, Cratchit and Co. reside in the Pierpont Morgan Library in New York to this day.

In his autobiography Hamilton Fish Armstrong, the editor and author born in New York City in 1893, left a poignant memory of his family's Christmas Eves. In his home wreaths were hung in all the windows and one was put around the front door knocker, covering all but the griffin's claw. "After dinner papa read the *Christmas Carol* aloud to the rest of the family in front of the fire downstairs. Everyone knew (as I did later) precisely what was in Scrooge's lumber room and could hear in advance world: Pickwick, David Copperfield, Fagin, Bill Sykes, Little Nell, Mr. Micawber, and a host of others. Some have insisted his characters are more like caricatures than finished portraits. Be that as it may, readers still respond warmly to Dickens' cast.

Likewise, *A Christmas Carol* introduces its share of memorable characters. Some of their names have even become part of our language. Take, for example, Ebenezer Scrooge. Can you think of a better name for a miser? We use his name to describe a tight-fisted individual: "He was a regular scrooge," we say. But Dickens puts it best when he introduces Scrooge to his readers:

Oh! But he was a tight-fisted hand at the grindstone, Scrooge! a squeezing, wrenching, grasping, scraping, clutching, coveteous old sinner! Hard and sharp as flint, from which no steel had ever struck out generous fire; secret, and self-contained, and solitary as an oyster.

It is hard not to dislike the man from the beginning. He starves and freezes his office clerk; he swears at his nephew who has simply stopped by to wish him a Merry Christmas; he refuses to make any charitable contribu-tions to the poor; he even frightens off a small boy who tries to sing a Christmas carol at the keyhole. Scrooge is a despicable man.

And yet as the story unfolds we do not come to hope Scrooge will "get his," but that he will change for the better. Dickens cleverly shows us the youthful Ebenezer deserted by everyone and left to spend Christmas at a boarding school. We also see what Scrooge sacrifices in his pursuit of money—the girl he once loved, a pleasant dinner with his nephew, and the warmth of human contact. So when the Ghost of Christmas Yet to Come reveals that Scrooge is destined to die in a bare bedroom with no one to mourn his passing, we rejoice to witness a repentant Scrooge and open our hearts to the changed man.

Tiny Tim is probably the second most popular character in the story. The crippled son of Scrooge's clerk, Bob Cratchit, Tiny Tim will die unless help comes to the struggling Cratchit family. The dear little fellow accompanies his father to church on Christmas Day in the hope that those who see him will be reminded of the one who made lame beggars walk and blind men see. The lad ends the story with those cheery words: "God Bless Us Every One!"

Page one from Dickens' original handwritten manuscript, now housed in the Pierpont Morgan Library. It reads: "Marley was dead: to begin with. There is no doubt whatever about that. The register of his burial was signed by the clergyman, the clerk, the undertaker, and the chief mourner. Scrooge signed it: and Scrooge's name was good upon 'Change, for anything he chose to put his hand to. Old Marley was as dead as a door-nail.

"Mind! I don't mean to say that I know, of my own knowledge, what there is particularly dead about a door-nail. I might have been inclined, myself, to regard a coffin-nail as the deadest piece of ironmongery in the trade. But the wisdom of our ancestors is in the simile; and my unhallowed hands shall not disturb it, or the Country's done for. You will therefore permit me to repeat, emphatically, that Marley was as dead as a door-nail.

"Scrooge knew he was dead? Of course he did. How could it be otherwise? Scrooge and he were partners for I don't know how many years. Scrooge was his sole executor, his sole administrator, his sole assign, his sole residuary legatee, his sole friend and sole mourner. And even Scrooge was not so dreadfully cut up by the sad event, but that he was an excellent man of business on the very day of the funeral, and solemnised it with an undoubted bargain. . . ."

And on Dickens goes, weaving a tale of humor, horror, and honor, to our continued delight.

15

Bob Cratchit, Scrooge's clerk, doesn't impress us as a very strong character. We wish he would, just once, tell off his miserly employer. Yet even at home and away from Scrooge, he still speaks gently about him. More to our liking is the bustling figure of Mrs. Cratchit as she prepares dinner for her numerous family. She worries about the goose and is almost too nervous to take out the pudding and bring it to the table. But when she enters, flushed and smiling proudly, her husband declares the pudding the greatest success achieved by Mrs. Cratchit since their marriage.

But when Bob Cratchit proposes a toast to "Mr. Scrooge, the Founder of the Feast," Mrs. Cratchit objects: "The Founder

Mr. Fezziwig's Ball by John Leech from the first edition.

of the Feast indeed! I wish I had him here. I'd give him a piece of my mind to feast upon, and I hope he'd have a good appetite for it." We feel like standing up and cheering for Mrs. Cratchit and all the faithful wives who suffer when their husbands are mistreated by employers. Mrs Cratchit is a gem.

Other endearing characters include Peter Cratchit, Scrooge's nephew, the pretty niece, the amorous Topper, Old Fezziwig, the rascals who steal Scrooge's possessions, and the ghost of Old Marley. More than 30 separate individuals are described in this short story. It is no wonder the material can be dramatized so easily; it contains such colorful roles.

Yet characters alone, whether

Memories of a Christmas Carol

PHILLIP SNYDER

In the 1940s and early 1950s, when I was growing up, our family of five and an equal number of relatives would gather around the radio in the living room on Christmas Eve to hear Lionel Barrymore read the part of Scrooge in Charles Dickens' *A Christmas Carol*. That time, not long after supper and before we left for church, was the most memorable part of a magical evening. My twin brother and I delighted to miss our normal bedtime.

Our radio was a capacious wooden console with a short-wave band. Hours earlier, while decorating the Christmas tree, we had listened to King George VI's Christmas message via the BBC. By the 1950s, if we were lucky and the atmospheric conditions were just right, we could pull in the prerecorded program from several successive time zones. Listening to Barrymore's hoarse, rasping voice harrumph and growl was a sublime, heart-warming tradition, marred in my memory only by the frustration of pawing gingerly about a darkened Christmas tree in search of the one burned-out bulb, which would inevitably, in the course of the evening, put out the entire tree.

The first of Barrymore's famous *Carol* broadcasts had been dramatized "live" from Hollywood to a rapturous nationwide audience on Christmas Day 1933. Over the years sponsors came and sponsors went, but Barrymore's presentation became a tradition. It would no doubt have pleased Lionel Barrymore to know the pleasure the memory of those programs has given me, boy and man. For he once said that, although he had played many roles, it was for the part of Ebenezer Scrooge he hoped to be remembered. He loved that squeezing, wrenching, grasping, scraping, clutching, covetous old sinner, not for what he was but for what he became—the converted

Scrooge who said humbly, "I will honour Christmas in my heart, and try to keep it all the year."

Lionel Barrymore was the Radio Age version of an old and fond Victorian custom now virtually lost, father's Christmas reading of Dickens' evocative ghost story. The Victorian family was never at a loss for things to do after dinner. There were games to play, songs to sing, recitations from the children (in Winchester, Virginia, in 1869 a boy learned 1,863 Bible verses during the year), and books to be read aloud.

Indeed, immediately upon the *Carol*'s publication in 1843, Dickens' friend John Foster wrote, "There poured upon (Dickens) daily, all through that Christmastime, letters from complete strangers to him, which I remember reading with a wonder of pleasure; not literary at all, but of the simplest domestic kind; of which the general burden was to tell him, amid many confidences, about their homes, how the *Carol* had come to be read aloud there and was to be kept upon a little shelf by itself, and was to do them no end of good."

On both sides of the Atlantic, the little book in its crimson and gold binding, with four illustrations by the Punch artist John Leech, appealed to rich and poor alike. Ultimately, the American financier John Pierpont Morgan bought Dickens' original manuscript. Old "J. P." used to have his librarian, Miss Belle da Costa Greene, read it to him every Christmas. And Scrooge, Cratchit and Co. reside in the Pierpont Morgan Library in New York to this day.

In his autobiography Hamilton Fish Armstrong, the editor and author born in New York City in 1893, left a poignant memory of his family's Christmas Eves. In his home wreaths were hung in all the windows and one was put around the front door knocker, covering all but the griffin's claw. "After dinner papa read the *Christmas Carol* aloud to the rest of the family in front of the fire downstairs. Everyone knew (as I did later) precisely what was in Scrooge's lumber room and could hear in advance amusing or entertaining or moving, do not make a great story. Behind the writing there should be some purpose, some moral principle, to guide the reader. *A Christmas Carol* paints a vivid moral lesson. Although not an orthodox Christian, Charles Dickens possessed a strong sense of right and wrong and was often upset at the injustice he saw. Scrooge represented for him people who are more concerned about profits than human lives. The old Scrooge expresses this view of life in his reply to those who come seeking a charitable contribution for the poor at Christmas: "It's enough for a man to understand his own business and not to interfere with other people's. Mine occupies me constantly."

Portrait of Charles Dickens at his desk by W. A. Frith.

This self-centered view is addressed by the ghost of Jacob Marley, Scrooge's dead business partner. Marley bitterly laments his former existence. In an effort to be comforting, Scrooge says, "But you were always a good man of business, Jacob." This elicits an even more sorrowful reply:

Business! Mankind was my business. The common welfare was my business; charity, mercy, forbearance, and benevolence, were, all, my business. The dealings of my trade were but a drop of water in the comprehensive ocean of my business!

Those words might form part of a sermon or an address to a labor union or to a meeting of employers. Dickens strikes hard at those who think only in terms

the potatoes knocking on the lid of Mrs. Cratchit's pot. Marion recommended that when Papa reached the place where the knocker changes into Marley's face you should visualize the griffin's tongue protruding from it; that would double the eeriness. Not one word has ever seemed stale to me and the lump rises in my throat impartially for Tiny Tim and for Little Scrooge alone in his schoolroom. Since the eighties, the initials of those gathered around the fire have been pencilled in the margin. At the start they filled the whole side of a page. Year by year, name by name, the list shortened."

Norman Rockwell never forgot the sound of his Victorian father reading Dickens by gaslight to his family in the evening. By 1904, 10-year-old Norman was already transforming the visions Dickens' words conjured up in his mind into pencil drawings. The Christmas 1934 *Saturday Evening Post* cover portraying Tiny Tim on Bob Cratchit's shoulders was one of the most popular of Rockwell's 25 Christmas covers for that magazine alone.

In 1944 at Hyde Park, New York, Radio Age or not, reading *A Christmas Carol* aloud was part of F.D.R.'s last Christmas. His son Elliot records the event: "The center table in the long room was pushed back, the Christmas tree was in place and decorated, the piles of presents were ready for unwrapping—each person's pile heaped on a separate chair. And on Christmas Eve Father took his accustomed rocker, to one side of the fireplace, and opened the familiar book, while we all found places around him. My place was prone on the floor by the grate. The fire crackled pleasantly; Father's voice, going over the well-remembered *Christmas Carol*, rose and fell rhythmically; my thoughts wandered, aimless, and presently ceased altogether. Then, jab! In my ribs came Faye's elbow and her fierce whisper in my ear: 'You were snoring! Sit up!' And I looked up sheepishly at Father, who only winked at me gravely and went on reading. I noticed that for some reason he had forgotten to put a false tooth in its place in the front of his lower

jaw. So, all of a sudden, did my nephew, Chris, Franklin Junior's three-year-old son. He leaned forward and in a clear voice interrupted Father's reading: 'Grandpère, you've lost a tooth!' It was a simple, direct statement, not requesting or requiring an answer, so Father smiled and went on reading. But all Chris' interest in *A Christmas Carol* was gone. Presently he stood up and walked over quite close to Father, leaned still closer, reached a

pointing finger within inches, and insisted, 'Grandpère, you've lost a tooth. Did you swallow it?'

"And that ended *A Christmas Carol* for that evening. 'There's too much competition in this family for reading aloud,' Father laughed and slammed shut the book."

Again this season, 142 years after the *Carol's* appearance, it will be read or quoted or, at least, recalled with affection in countless homes. In one home with which I'm acquainted it will still be read aloud.

Bob Cratchit and Tiny Tim on the cover of *The Saturday Evening Post*.

of profit and loss and who pass by the needy and the unfortunate of this world. Marley emphasizes his point in reference to Christmas:

> At this time of the rolling year I suffer most. Why did I walk through the crowds of fellow-beings with my eyes turned down, and never raise them to that blessed Star which led the Wise Men to a poor abode? Were there no poor homes to which its light would have conducted *me*!

This sense of loss because he didn't act when he had the opportunity is the dominating thought behind Marley's words and action. He lost his chance seven years ago, but his ghost has come to see if something can be done for Scrooge before it is too late. When Marley leaves, Scrooge goes to the window and sees other ghosts floating through the air, all linked to emblems of their business. One whom Scrooge recognizes, an old man in a white waistcoat, is crying piteously because he wants to assist a young woman with an infant but cannot do so. Dickens writes: "The misery with them all was, clearly, that they sought to interfere, for good, in human matters, and had lost the power forever." The message of Jesus, that we must work while it is day because the night comes when no one can work, is clearly stressed.

Although the ghosts do not preach to Scrooge or make any effort to change him, the picture of Scrooge's transformation from a nasty creature to a caring individual recalls to mind the conversion of a sinner. Note the language Dickens uses to indicate what has happened. Scrooge awakens after his visit in the spirit world and is so excited he can scarcely dress himself:

Dickens' house on 48 Doughty Street, London, is now a museum.

I don't know what to do! I am as light as a feather. I am as happy as an angel. I am as merry as a schoolboy. I am as giddy as a drunken man . . . I don't know what day of the month it is! I don't know anything. I'm quite a baby. Never mind, I don't care. I'd rather be a baby.

This is an excellent description of a person changed by the power of the Holy Spirit, even though Dickens does not use that kind of language. It makes us glow with satisfaction just to hear Scrooge talk. What a contrast he is to the cross old bear in the first part of the story!

Nor is this just a temporary conversion, an emotional jag brought on by disturbing dreams. Scrooge acts on his new resolutions. He sends the Cratchit family a large turkey for their Christmas dinner. He gives money for charity to the man he had scorned the day before. He goes to Christmas dinner at the home of his nephew, the young man he had driven away from his office. Scrooge even raises Bob Cratchit's pay, an action that almost makes the poor clerk think his employer has lost his mind. Best of all, Scrooge becomes a second father to Tiny Tim, who does not die. Thus Dickens assures us that the change of heart is permanent. In fact, we are told at the end of the story that Scrooge "knew how to keep Christmas well, if any man alive possessed the knowledge."

Few writers possess the keen humor, warm humanity, and strong moral sense of a Charles Dickens. Perhaps that is why the story of one crusty old man's rejuvenated heart continues to draw new admirers. Surely that is a great accomplishment. Dickens' carol in prose still speaks to a world that can use all the examples of love it can find. What more can we say than to echo the prayer of the convicted Scrooge: "I will honour Christmas in my heart, and try to keep it all the year."

Christmas in Victoria

NANCY VIGNEC

Set sail for Victoria. Ferry across the strait separating Vancouver Island from mainland British Columbia. Dock in Victoria's Inner Harbour, as did the early explorers and settlers long ago. Then step ashore to discover in Victoria's Christmas celebration the traditions of Old England interpreted with New World exuberance.

In the Inner Harbour, *The Princess Marguerite* with Union Jacks blazoned on her smokestacks is anchored for the winter. Sailboats with Christmas trees on deck bob on the waves nearby. Red double-decker London buses drive past totem poles carved by the island's original inhabitants.

Fur trade with neighboring Nootka Indians marked the city's early years as Fort Victoria, a frontier outpost for the Hudson Bay Company. British officers and colonial officials who settled here indulged their fondness for formal gardens and high tea and cultivated Victoria's distinctive English character.

To visualize Christmas in an early Victoria home, visit Helmcken house, British Columbia's oldest residence still in its original form. This white clapboard building was the home of Dr. John Helmcken, who came to Fort Victoria in 1850 as the Hudson Bay Company physician.

Photo: Glittering Parliament Buildings reflected in the harbor.

Among the original furnishings in Helmcken House is the dining room table, which doubled as an operating platform in emergencies. At Christmas the table was set for 20 or more guests, Dr. Helmcken's extended family, who feasted in true English style. Appetizers of oyster patties and soup gave way to the main course of roast turkey, goose, chicken, ham, and tongue, followed by platters of vegetables, then flaming plum pudding, mince tarts, and an assortment of fruits.

Christmas evening festivities continued with a round of toasts saluting the queen and all those seated at the table. Then the candle-studded Christmas tree was lighted, and dancing began, lasting long into the night.

Other scenes from Victoria's past are recreated in the Provincial Museum where you may stand on the after-deck of Captain James Cook's *HMS Discovery*, feel the roll and pitch of the ocean waves, and listen to the wail of seagulls. Next, sniff the pungent spices of an early settler's farm kitchen and the scent of fresh cut cedar in a backcountry sawmill. Hear ceremonial chanting in an Indian longhouse. Climb down a mine shaft to see a coal mine, then go on to a gold miner's camp. Stroll the boardwalk of a turn-of-the-century street past the Grand Hotel, the Roxy Theatre (featuring black and white "flickers"), and the railway station where a telegraph clicks out a message in Morse code.

Coal mines, lumber mills, steamships, and railways formed the financial empire of Robert Dunsmuir, whose mansion, Craigdarroch Castle, was built over 90 years ago in Victoria. The castle's exterior facade was constructed of grey sandstone. It peaks in towers, spires, turrets, and chimneys. The inside walls are panelled with quarter-cut golden oak; the floors are marble or intricate inlay mosaics of rosewood, ebony, oak, and maple. In the double drawing room, the flower motif of the leaded glass windows is repeated by the scarlet poinsettias placed on the tables at Christmastime.

Christmas window shopping in Victoria's Inner Harbour area provides another glimpse of the city's heritage. Tartans from Scotland, weavings from Wales, English bone china, British woolens, and Harris tweeds are displayed in small shops, some established 75 to 100 years ago.

More than three generations of Victoria residents have selected teas blended at Murchies. Here spices stored in glass apothecary jars and blends of coffee or tea scooped from red and gold tin cannisters and bins are weighed on old-fashioned scales.

Visitors to Roger's chocolate shop may sample the original Victoria Creams, a specialty since 1885, and enjoy the shop's late Victorian decor of oak walls and fixtures, stained glass windows, and Italian lights.

The essence of nineteenth century masculinity pervades Old Morris Tobacconists, where "smoker's requisites" have been sold since 1892. At Christmastime silver bunting and red ribbons festoon the shop's original mahogany fittings. Walls lined with London pipes, counters displaying Havana cigars and jars of tobacco, and the central free-standing Mexican onyx cigar lighter contribute to the ambience.

Inside Crabtree and Evelyn, purveyors to the gentry, Christmas fragrances mingle. Seasonal specialties include spice sachets used in mulling wine; packets of Noel potpourri (a blend of pine cones, juniper berries, cedar needles, and orange peel); and red currant, apple, or herbal jellies, historically called "tracklements," to accompany the Christmas turkey.

Photos: Craigdarroch Castle; Roger's chocolate shop; Crabtree and Evelyn; Old Morris Tobacconists.

Subtle signs of Christmas accent storefront windows. The Irish Linen Store features table runners and placemats embroidered with holly leaves and berries. At Sydney Reynolds China Shop a Wise Man seated on a camel forms the centerpiece of a figurine display.

In Victoria's Market Square, a quadrangle of historic buildings constructed between 1894 and 1900, holiday shoppers pause to hear costumed carollers and strolling minstrels present Christmas melodies. Baaing sheep, the seasonal occupants of a courtyard manger scene, provide the accompaniment.

Several members of the outdoor audience wear sweaters of bold grey, white, and black design. These warm, durable, and naturally water-repellant sweaters are handmade of raw wool by Indians of Vancouver Island's Cowichan River area.

Ever since its completion early in the twentieth century, the Empress Hotel has dominated Victoria's Inner Harbour. Admired for her prominence and longevity, the Empress is affectionately called Victoria's Dowager. At teatime this ivy-covered Edwardian chateau personifies a gracious, utterly self-assured hostess staging a vast tea party.

High tea—a substantial meal of crumpets, scones, finger sandwiches, and cakes—is served at damask-clothed tables set up in the spacious lobby. The teatime crowd may include the society matron, the wide-eyed tourist, and the confirmed eccentric. (Artist Emily Carr took tea here accompanied by her pet monkey in its pram.)

The lobby's potted palms and ornate Doric columns are its indisputably dominant fixtures, even at Christmas when a lighted evergreen is tucked in one corner of the room. Greens grace the fireplace mantel. Snowberries and poinsettias are brought in from the hotel's greenhouse for the season. Subdued, harmonious Christmas decorations at the Empress create a genteel, inviting holiday atmosphere.

Preference for an elegantly subtle Christmas decorating scheme seems to prevail throughout Victoria, especially when viewed in daylight. But as evening skies darken, amiable understatement gives way to equally delightful extravagance in Victoria's Christmas lighting display.

The city's residential areas, famed for their quiet streets, trim lawns, and stately gardens, are transformed in a blaze of holiday illumination. Rooflines, doorways, and windows are outlined with glowing lights. Decorated homes resemble gingerbread houses or fairy castles. Groups of spotlighted figures present the nativity scene or Santa and his reindeer.

Illuminated to suggest a glittering tiara against a black velvet backdrop, Victoria's Parliament Buildings crown the city's Christmas lighting display. The 3,564 tiny white lights outlining the buildings' entire facade were first lit to commemorate Queen Victoria's Diamond Jubilee. On the front lawn, a giant sequoia growing near the statue of young Queen Victoria is laden with colored lights.

Her Majesty's naval fleet, anchored in Esquimalt Harbour, joins the exuberant lighting display. Crews hoist evergreens to the top of shipmasts and string colored lights from stem to stern. Then the public is invited for a show of luminous ship images glimmering across the harbour waters.

Visitors to this area of Victoria may discover in Esquimalt an access to Merrie Olde England. A half-timbered, gabled Tudor mansion, the Olde England Inn, offers a selection of such English dishes as steak and kidney pie, roast beef, and Yorkshire pudding. Christmas dinner in the inn's Baronial Hall is a festive pageant, presented by costumed *serviteurs* and scullions. Beamed ceilings, a copper-hooded fireplace, and Elizabethan jousting armor set the stage.

An authentic view of everyday life in long-ago England is realized in Anne Hathaway's cottage, an exact replica of the childhood home of William Shakespeare's wife. The cottage is an irregular, half-timbered building with diamond-paned lattice windows and a thatched roof.

Inside, hand-adzed timbers beam the ceilings. A guide describes sixteenth century use of the household equipment and furnishings. The detailed depiction of old English customs is fascinating, but the tour of Anne Hathaway's cottage also reveals that life in Merrie Olde England was not entirely comfortable by contemporary standards. In the upstairs bedchambers, overnight guests slept huddled together on a rush-covered floor. The parents' four-poster bed was furnished with a rope mattress in an era 100 years before feather mattresses were introduced.

While Victoria's past is clearly linked with England, the origins of its present-day population may be traced round the globe. In the weeks before Christmas, traditional dances of Hungary, Mexico, the Ukraine, the Philippines, and the Netherlands are performed. The Balalaika Orchestra plays, and *Sinterklaus* comes to town.

Dressed in a flowing red robe and mitre, *Sinterklaus*, the Dutch interpretation of Saint Nicholas, sails into Victoria's Inner Harbour in early December. His arrival is marked by ringing of the Netherlands Centennial Carillon, a speech by Victoria's mayor, and a parade through the city.

During the Christmas season Victoria's churches and theaters stage numerous holiday plays and recitals. The selection of Christmas concerts ranges from pop medley to classical symphony. A sing-along *Messiah* attracts enthusiastic participation.

On Christmas morning, the bells of Christ Church Cathedral peal throughout downtown Victoria. Christ Church, constructed in thirteenth century Gothic design, is the oldest of British Columbia's Anglican churches. The pulpit is made from a 500-year-old English oak tree and the choir screen came from London's Westminster Abbey. The vaulted ceiling resounds with Christmas music from an organ of 3000 pipes.

An Elizabethan-style Christmas dinner is a popular feature at several Victoria hotels and inns. Victoria's Dowager reigns as favorite among Christmas visitors to the city.

At the Empress Hotel an Elizabethan Christmas celebration has been the tradition for 65 years. Guests are awakened Christmas morning by madrigal singers who parade through the hotel corridors performing medieval carols. The evening celebration begins with a Yule log procession led by a capering jester dressed in a half-red, half-green tunic, and a belled cap, followed by a trumpeter and seneschal

Photos: The Inner Harbour; musicians on the dock; *Sinterklaus;* Queen's Pipers in the Christmas Parade.

clothed in purple and mauve. A steward pours vintage wine and drippings from the Christmas turkey over the Yule log, a three-by-four foot piece of cedar, before lighting it with a splinter saved from last year's log. (Secretly storing a Yule log splinter beneath a hotel resident's bed from one year to the next is an Empress tradition believed to ensure good luck in the coming year.) The Christmas proclamation is read; then the guests delve into a seven-course Christmas dinner. Between courses, chefs parade through the dining room carrying a decorated boar's head, a Yule log formed from 40 pounds of lard, a turkey in full plumage, and a sugar and icing church.

The day after Christmas is a Canadian holiday known as Boxing Day. Boxing Day originated in England long ago; several explanations for the holiday are offered. One tradition points to the English practice of opening church alms boxes on the day after Christmas and distributing the contents to needy parish families. Others suggest that gifts for the servants may have come in wooden boxes, which were returned to the stores on the day after Christmas.

Many Victorians prefer to spend Boxing Day in celebration of the city's surprisingly mild winter climate. Protected by mountain ranges and warmed by the Japanese current, Kuroshio, Victoria is spared the wintry weather of most Canadian cities. On Boxing Day, while much of Canada lies buried in snow drifts, Victorians play golf in an annual tournament known as the "Christmas Tee."

Nongolfers may celebrate Boxing Day with a stroll in Beacon Hill Park. High on a bluff, the park overlooks the headlands and rugged beaches of Juan de Fuca Strait and provides an excellent vantage point for the snow-capped Olympic Mountains of Washington State. Blazing fires were lighted here at one time to guide mariners into the harbor. A 127-foot totem pole stands sentry in the park as monument to a treasured artistic heritage and symbol of Canada's native peoples.

On Boxing Day, and throughout

Photos: Ship decked out for Christmas; traditional boar's head carried in procession; Empress Hotel; Las Posadas.

the winter, mallards, gulls, and shovelers crowd the wildfowl sanctuary at Beacon Hill's Goodacre Lake. Beacon Hill swans come from Her Majesty Queen Elizabeth's Swannery at Cookham-on-Thames, England. Feeding flocks of fowl is a pastime popular with park visitors.

Victoria, the Garden City, is famed for its spring flowering bulbs, summer floral displays, and rose gardens. In December seeds for the city's flower planters, window boxes, and hanging baskets are started in Beacon Hill Park Greenhouses. During the winter months the planters accenting city sidewalks and street corners are bright with primroses.

Exotic colors complement Christmas hues inside Victoria's glass-roofed Crystal Garden. Poinsettias and tropical foliage line walkways and terraces. Pink flamingos stand near ponds where Japanese carp and goldfish swim. Azure parrots, macaws, and toucans enhance the multi-colored array.

Natural reds and greens of the Christmas season color landscaped gardens surrounding Victoria's Government House. Low growing evergreens nestle among outcroppings of exposed rock spread with red-berried cotoneaster. Blue-green spruce and verdant pine form a multitiered background.

A California redwood dominates the main entrance to the Government House, official residence of the Lieutenant-Governor. On New Year's Day each year the Lieutenant-Governor, the Queen's representative to the people of British Columbia, invites the general public to a reception, or levee. Victoria residents attending the New Year's Day levee share Christmas greetings and best wishes for the New Year with their mayor, Lieutenant-Governor, and elected officials.

Guests at the Government House may contemplate a New Year's Day vista of British Columbia's capital city. The regal ballroom commands an extensive overview of Victoria, "the last bastion of the English Empire," home port for the New World adventurer and the Old World traditionalist. Such is Victoria, a city whose Christmas festivities are as delightfully distinctive, carefully blended, and warmly refreshing as a steaming cup of good English tea.

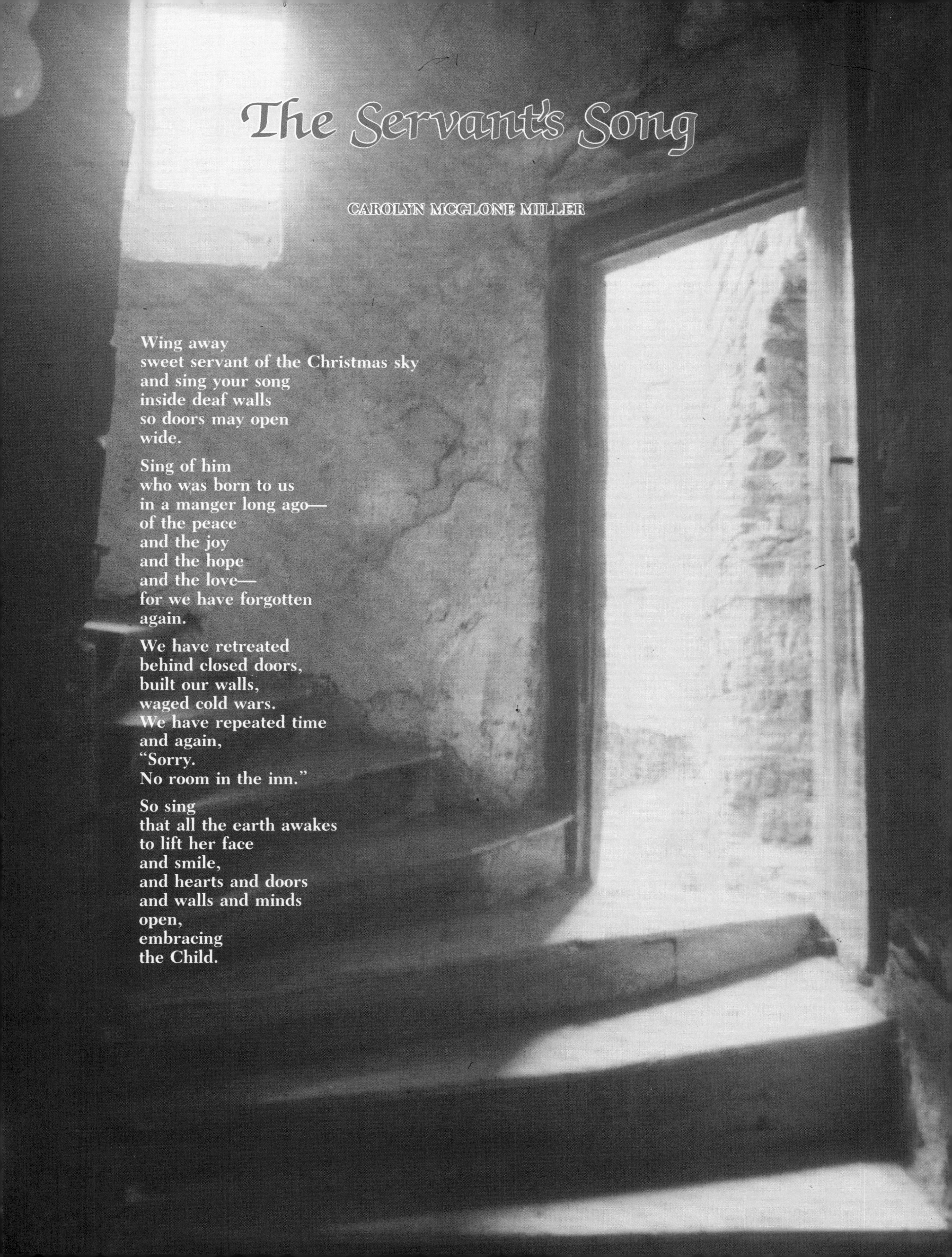

The Servant's Song

CAROLYN MCGLONE MILLER

Wing away
sweet servant of the Christmas sky
and sing your song
inside deaf walls
so doors may open
wide.

Sing of him
who was born to us
in a manger long ago—
of the peace
and the joy
and the hope
and the love—
for we have forgotten
again.

We have retreated
behind closed doors,
built our walls,
waged cold wars.
We have repeated time
and again,
"Sorry.
No room in the inn."

So sing
that all the earth awakes
to lift her face
and smile,
and hearts and doors
and walls and minds
open,
embracing
the Child.

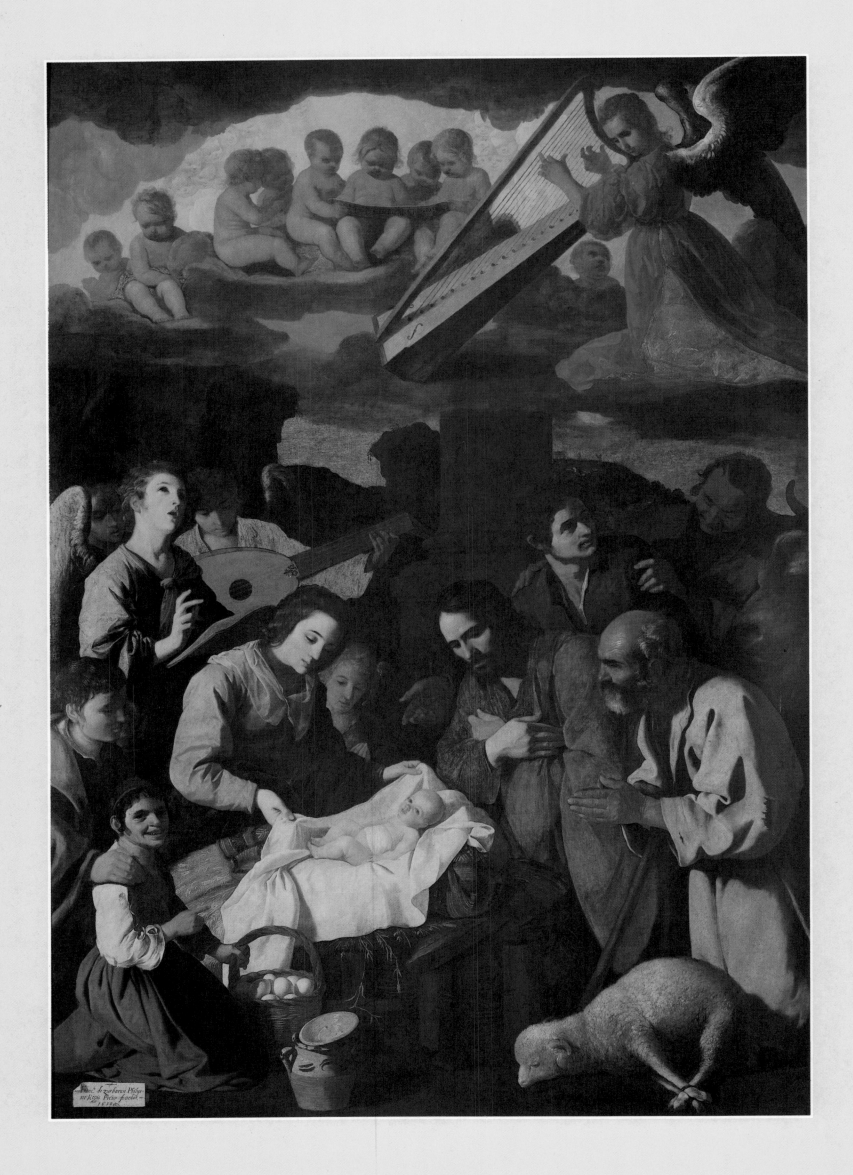

Adoration of the Shepherds

Francisco de Zurbarán, 1598-1664

PHILLIP GUGEL

Of the hundreds of versions of this subject by Renaissance and Baroque painters, Zurbarán's altarpiece is one of the more imaginative. His richly colored composition with its serene figures leads us, as it led the Carthusian monks who hired him to paint it, to soberly meditate on the meaning of our Savior's birth.

Seemingly oblivious of his visitors, the infant Jesus is more interested in glancing out at us to make contact; his interest in us makes him personal and is an invitation to enter his world. Subtilely detailed down to the creases in his skin, the babe's features and his exquisitely done swaddling cloth show Zurbarán's skill in painting human features and drapery.

Lest we become too sentimental about this winsome babe, Zurbarán placed two reminders of God's destiny for him nearby. The stalks of wheat for his mattress signify that Jesus is the bread of life, an important eucharistic theme in John's gospel. The bound sacrificial lamb, with its exquisitely painted wool coat, connects him to the Passover lamb and proclaims that he is the *Agnus Dei*, the Lamb of God, a title given him also in John's gospel by John the Baptist, who proclaims Jesus' mission.

Mary's gesture of uncovering her son lead these obscure sheep-tenders to become the first to recognize him as Savior. According to one scholar, this detail has been part of many nativity paintings since 1550. Joseph, who kneels with his arms and hands crossed in devotion, and Mary are less animated than their visitors as they ponder this child's presence.

Light from the left bathes most figures, fully illuminating the infant, but striking the others at various angles to produce dramatic contrasts of light and shadow on their faces and clothing.

As she points to the babe it seems as if the shepherdess is inviting us to come, see, and adore him as well. Her gesture, along with her glance and smile at us activates the scene and draws us into it. Her friendly and joyous look is accented by the bright vermilion color of her skirt with its well-painted folds. The gaps between her teeth, her homely face, and her torn sleeve show that Zurbarán did not idealize the peasant figures he painted, an approach he shared with his peers Jusepe de Ribera and Diego Velázquez. Their sensitive portrayals of ordinary Spanish folk gave them dignity and serenity despite any imperfections. Nor, as Zurbarán showed in his depiction of the sturdy young shepherd resting his hand affectionately on the shoulder of the shepherdess, were these persons without affection for each other.

Her wicker basket with its gift of eggs, the ceramic pitcher and saucer, the manger's wooden and wicker surfaces, the stalks of wheat, and the woven rug cushioning the babe are examples of Zurbarán's masterful depiction of the colors and textures of material objects, as well as the play of light upon them.

Perhaps Zurbarán wanted to fool us when he painted his skillful imitation of a strip of paper, with one bent corner casting a shadow, on the lower left corner of his canvas. Its inscription tells us that he was "Painter to the King," a title he received from Philip the Third of Spain, and that the *Adoration* was executed in 1638.

The elderly shepherd on the right with his grizzled hair, deeply tanned face, rough wrinkled hands folded in devotion, and torn tunic with its carefully shadowed folds, is another example of Zurbarán's appealing portraiture of peasants. Next to the ox behind him, the gestures and glances exchanged by his other two companions contrast his rapt figure.

Though the shepherds worship the babe in silence, his heavenly visitors praise him with voices and stringed instruments as Psalm 150 directs. Since the seventeenth century was a golden age for lute music, Zurbarán's inclusion of one, ornamented with an inlaid rosette and strummed by a phosphorescently-gowned angel, reminds us of its popularity as a Baroque instrument.

A small background zone, serving as a transitional area for Zurbarán's merger of earthly and heavenly regions on this canvas, shows a shadowy column and ruins, symbolic of the Old Testament's messianic prophecies now fulfilled by Jesus' birth and by the angel's announcement.

A diagonal line, beginning with the shepherdess and ending with the harpist, helps unite the babe's earthly and heavenly visitors, as does the angelic singer with upraised eyes. The faces of the angel soloist and the kneeling companion are delicately done and set off by their vivid green gowns.

Above, the harping angel dominates, attired in a bright rose gown and multihued wings. The harp has a sounding board with two rare f-shaped perforations and is smaller than its modern counterpart. Zurbarán's careful rendition of it and the angel's face and hands demonstrate his skillful technique.

The wispy-haired, chubby cherubs sharing their music sheets are charming additions; several chorus members seem distracted elsewhere like anyone their age. They add a touch of humor to Zurbarán's picture. If you look carefully at the warm hues of the clouds above and behind them, you will see the faces of a much larger cherubic chorus traced in them.

Its figures, artificially arranged as if onstage, merge space and time in their setting. Lost in contemplation and praise, they reflect Zurbarán's sense of human dignity, quiet joy, and faith in God who came among us.

The Bach Legend Lives

Johann Sebastian Bach, 1685-1750

ROBERT E. A. LEE

There was music in the house 300 years ago when the newest Bach baby, Johann Sebastian, experienced his first Christmas. The Bach clan was peopled with music makers—fiddlers, organists, trumpeters, and drummers. Sebastian's father, Johann Ambrosius, was the town piper. His duties included playing at community functions and playing before and after the sermon in the Lutheran worship services.

The town was Eisenach, Germany, where the spirit of Martin Luther was ever present. Nearby towered Wartburg Castle, famous as the place where Luther translated the New Testament into German. Luther's spirit was audible, too. His hymn tunes and texts were part of the environment, especially at Christmas!

Vom Himmel Hoch ("From heaven above") by Luther surely was sung and played and drummed into the infant Sebastian's consciousness that first Christmas of his life. Later he would harmonize the tune, play with it contrapuntally, fashion it fugally, set it for organ and orchestra and chorus, and even weave it into a musical puzzle (*Canonic Variations*).

Nine months before Christmas, on March 21, 1685, Sebastian had been born into that musical family. His mother died when he was only nine,

Portrait of Bach by Elias Gottlieb Haussmann.

followed by his father less than a year later. The orphan, Johann Sebastian, was assigned to the care of an older brother, Johann Christoph, who was organist in the town of Ohrdruf about 30 miles from Eisenach. Christoph had been a pupil of Pachelbel at Erfurt and had assembled a library of music that included some of the baroque masters. These works Sebastian could now experience at first hand and assimilate into his own already astounding musical consciousness. Christoph became both foster father and music teacher. Legend has it that he punished

his ward after discovering that his precious manuscripts had been purloined one by one from a locked music cabinet. Sebastian had taken them to copy at night by moonlight!

Little did Christoph know that he was helping to launch the career of the greatest musical genius the world would ever know! Sebastian went on to study at a choir school at Lüneburg; play violin in the Duke's band at Weimar; become an organist at Mühlhausen, at Arnstadt, and again at Weimar; serve as court composer at Cöthen; and, finally, spend the last 27 years of his life as director of music in the city of Leipzig and as cantor of St. Thomas church and school.

Bach's musical monuments include hundreds of church cantatas (along with some secular ones), plus passions, oratorios, chorales, motets, concertos, chamber music, and dozens of organ and other keyboard works —chorale preludes, preludes and fugues, fantasies, variations, suites. His musical legacy extends all the way from simple songs to complex formulations such as *The Musical Offering* and *The Art of the Fugue*.

Bach wrote both Advent and Christmas cantatas when he worked for Duke Wilhelm Ernst at Weimar between 1708 and 1717. The organ loft was high in a balcony room three stories above the altar in the castle church called the *Himmelsburg*. One can imagine the royal family at Christmas listening to Bach's music wafting down "from heaven above." In that setting the text from Luke's gospel would have become almost audiovisually literal.

Over the altar canopy a Baroque obelisk reached heavenward. On it, surrounding a painting, were eight dancing cherubs that appeared to be floating in the air. While hearing Bach's organ elaborating the theme of "From heaven above to earth I come," the worshipers could in fantasy "see" the almost animated cherubs descending with the good news!

Advent cantatas (except for the First Sunday in Advent) were not required in Leipzig during the time Bach wrote church music there, beginning in 1723. The period of four weeks was called *tempus clausum* and, like Lent, was draped by a curtain of silence as a way of inspiring penitence.

But at the Christmas festival in Leipzig Bach was permitted to "pull out all the stops," which he frequently did. He would call for the trumpets and the tympani. He would find ever new ways musically to evoke joy and celebration. And he would at the same time depict the rocking of a cradle as a rhythmic accompaniment to a lullaby for the baby Jesus or would suggest the gentle loping of shepherds in a siciliano with a 6/8 beat.

The very first Christmas in Leipzig he introduced his setting of *The Magnificat* at vespers. The congregation must have been stunned. The 12-part, 20-minute work is framed by sections featuring celebratory trumpets and tympani. These instruments set the mood for joy and for praise as they always do in Bach's music. The five-part chorus repetitively voices the key word, *magnificat*, from Mary's canticle: "My soul doth magnify the Lord" (or in a contemporary version, "My soul proclaims the greatness of the Lord"). The singers play with that key word. They let it roll out, one part after the other; they articulate it forcefully in a common chordal shout; and they act out the happy excitement of Mary's response to the angel's announcement (Luke 1:46).

The Magnificat is both vigorous and delicate, both exuberant and pensive. The Latin phrases become individual works. *Omnes generationes*, for example, starts with the chorus bursting in over the final note of the previous aria in which the soprano sings about Mary's being called blessed by "all generations." A kind of race through history is presented as five different chorus voices imitate one another every half-measure through almost the entire number. They conclude with a brilliant canon in which the voices are telescoped even more closely together. There is an incomparable eagerness and zest in this word painting that finds the voices flinging the word *omnes* from one part to another, while the continuo throbs underneath.

Perhaps the major Christmas legend arising out of Bach's prodigious composing career is the background story of his producing *The Christmas Oratorio* in 1734.

Bach was at a pivotal point in his career that year. He was restless. He was a man of 49 years, the last 11 of which had been spent in Leipzig. He sent out a poignant probe in 1730 in the form of a letter to a boyhood friend, hoping for a new position. It didn't come.

He may have had the equivalent 250 years ago of today's so-called "burnout." He no longer composed a weekly cantata for church services unless it was a special occasion. He contented himself by drawing on his library. After all, between 1723 and 1728 he had created a massive musical menu of church cantatas more than matching the agenda of biblical texts over a cycle of three years. When repeating these in the 1730s, he would often make minor or major revisions. (When updating *The Magnificat*, for example, he added instruments and changed the entire work into the key of D from the original E flat.)

But it was more than his being tired and weary. He was undergoing a midlife crisis. It comes to many persons as they nudge the half-century mark. A new boss comes in bringing a clean broom! New ideas. Rumors of changes. The old staff begins to think the new chief does not appreciate them.

Parlor of Bach's childhood home in Eisenach features a portrait of his father, Johann Ambrosius.

So it was with the Leipzig cantor. He had had a wonderful relationship with Johannes Gesner, the former rector of the St. Thomas school. The two men had seen themselves as equals before the town council, even though technically Gesner was administrative head of the school. They had even shared a love for music. Then Gesner was offered a position he couldn't refuse—a professorship at the University of Göttengen. Bach gave him a going-away present that bespoke musically their mutual respect: a perpetual two-part canon, a musical puzzle.

Gesner has given us in a letter one of the best contemporary reports that we have of Bach in action. It could only come from a friend who had observed him closely on many occasions:

You (should) see him not only singing with one voice and playing his own parts, but watching over everything and bringing back to the rhythm and the beat, out of 30 or even 40 musicians, the one with a nod, another by tapping with his foot, the third with a warning finger, giving the right note to one from the top of his voice, to another from the bottom, and to a third from the middle of it—all alone, in the midst of the greatest din made by all the participants, and, although he is executing the most difficult parts himself, noticing at once whenever or wherever a mistake occurs, holding everyone together, taking precautions everywhere, and repairing any unsteadiness, full of rhythm in every part of his body—this one man taking in all these harmonies with his keen ear and emitting with his voice alone the tone of all the voices.

Suddenly Gesner was gone and a new rector was installed. Bach knew this man who had been promoted

Bach and Ernesti tangled soon after. The new rector let it be known that he didn't plan to coddle musicians at the school. Karl Geiringer, in his excellent book, *Johann Sebastian Bach*, points out that the young rector, in his ambition to create an outstanding institute of learning, "saw in the students' musical duties nothing but an obstacle to the fulfillment of his plans." That was the beginning of the battle between Bach and Ernesti.

This was the same Ernesti whose educational philosophy helped usher in the neo-humanist ideas associated with the age of rationalism. Earlier, orthodox Lutheran that he was, Bach had resisted the pressures of pietism in Mülhausen. Now he would even more staunchly resist what he would surely consider a dangerous and almost heretical new teaching. The ensuing feud between Bach and Ernesti became nasty; Bach ultimately called upon the king to settle it.

Bach was uncomfortable, unhappy, unappreciated, and, as a result, increasingly cantankerous. But through it all he had his professional integrity to maintain. And he had his family responsibilities to fulfill. His second wife, Anna Magdalena, had come to Leipzig as a new bride and had borne ten children in those eleven years. Only three survived for the Christmas of 1734, together with three sons and a daughter from Bach's previous marriage to Maria Barbara. (Maria had died in Cöthen in 1720 while her husband was at Carlsbad entertaining Prince Leopold and his entourage.)

Throughout this time of tension and emotional *Sturm und Drang*, Sebastian faced the weekly obligation to prepare music for the three churches in Leipzig. He had organists assisting him and a cadre of town musicians who provided the instrumental foundation for his choral works. But Christmas was coming and the music for it required special attention and planning.

First, however, came the famous Leipzig *Messe* or annual fair. It brought tourists and tradespeople

Interior of St. Thomas Church in Leipzig, one of four churches for which Bach served as music director and cantor.

from vice-principal of the St. Thomas school. He was Johann August Ernesti. Because he was 22 years Bach's junior, Sebastian had probably dismissed him earlier as an upstart. Now this 27-year old was Bach's equal and—awful thought—his administrative superior. His boss!

Sebastian started out on the right foot by composing and performing a welcoming cantata at Ernesti's installation. The text has been preserved and it is (we dare not think intentionally) truly banal. (The music, except for a borrowed aria from a 1725 cantata, has been lost.)

from far and near. In October of 1734 it also brought the royal family from Dresden. This was a time, too, of political change, and Leipzigers were eager to show the new king, Augustus III of Poland, and his retinue that they knew how to produce a royal welcome. Naturally, the city's director of music would be expected to provide the musical entertainment.

Bach proved an adequate showman. In fact, he came through triumphantly. With the help of university students and others, he performed his own work, *Preise dein Glücke, gesegnetes Sachsen*, as a royal salute. An account published at the time describes the scene:

> In the evening at seven a cannon was fired and the whole town was illuminated. . . . At about nine in the evening the resident students humbly presented a serenade with trumpets and drums to his majesty, composed by Mr. Joh. Bach, capellmeister and cantor at St. Thomas. Six hundred students carried wax torches, and four counts acted as marshals, leading the music. . . . When the composition was presented, the four counts were graciously permitted to kiss his majesty's hand. The King, the Queen, and the Princess did not leave the window but listened to the music with great pleasure as long as it lasted.

Bach's close friend, trumpeter Gottfried Reiche, was an indirect casualty of the king's visit. He had been in the town square playing in Bach's orchestra for the little opera (called *Dramma per Musica*) and had elegantly executed the shrill trumpet flourishes the composer had known Reiche could play. But the exertion may have been too much for him as he had a stroke and died the following day. In his official portrait the musician is shown holding his spiral trumpet and the music for the Reiche flourish.

There is evidence that Bach was under considerable personal and professional pressure when he planned the Christmas music for 1734. Nevertheless he and his librettist outlined an ambitious work. They called it an oratorio, but it was in reality a package of six cantatas intended to be serially performed beginning on Christmas Day and continuing one part on each of the following days: Second Day of Christmas, Third Day of Christmas, New Year's Day (Festival of the Circumcision), the Sunday after New Year's Day, and the Feast of the Epiphany. Considering the pressure under which Bach was struggling, he could have attempted something simpler. But, his pride and professional integrity were at stake. Besides, he must have wanted to make an impression on those who had the ear of Ernesti, if not on the new rector himself.

Bach the Borrower recycled choruses and arias from his other works in order to flesh out these six half-hour performances under the German title, *Weihnachts Oratorium*. The printed program states that they were to be "performed musically in two principal churches of Leipzig during the sacred festival of Christmas." The program also reveals that on Christmas Day the morning

performance was at the St. Nicolai Church (one of the four churches in the town for which Bach supplied music) and the afternoon performance at the St. Thomas church.

In addition to using one aria from the production prepared for the king, heard in Leipzig less than three months earlier, he borrowed from two other secular works. Sebastian liked the idea, apparently, of using secular works dedicated to royalty as the basis for religious works dedicated to God. He clearly had the enthusiastic collaboration of librettist Picander, the pen name for Christian Friedrich Henrici, a postal official who provided new texts for the old melodies. After all, he had written the original texts, too.

They borrowed freely from their earlier work in honor of Prince Friedrich of Saxony, *Hercules at the Crossroads*, performed the previous year in September. The grand opening for the oratorio came from the birthday cantata for the Crown Princess, presented in December 1733, *Beat, Kettle Drums; Blow, Trumpets*. And three other solos and choruses came from the same source.

Together Bach and Picander did a quick cut-and-paste job to augment the new work they had composed and

In a career that often brought him before royalty, Bach performed for Frederich the Great at Potsdam.

authored. Somehow, genius prevailed, and it all seemed to hang together with logic and beauty and cohesion. And, as we now know, it has stood the test of 250 years and more.

The last Christmas of Bach's life was in December of 1749. By then he was 64 years of age chronologically, but much older than that physically. He was feeble, frail, and blind.

The Leipzig authorities did not wait for him to die. They appointed his successor while he was still alive—

an ignominious gesture for one who had dedicated his life to the people of that community.

Nevertheless, Johann Sebastian Bach continued to create music almost to the very end, in spite of his blindness. He had the good assistance of a former pupil, Christoph Altnikol, who had married Bach's daughter Elizabeth. Bach dictated to his son-in-law, a collaboration which produced the profound musical architecture called *The Art of the Fugue*. It ends with Bach's own signature in music hidden within it.

Bach had a mind that loved the mystery and challenge connected with puzzles and mathematical or geometric connections to harmonic and contrapuntal structures. So, when Bach applied for a membership in the Association for Musical Science, established by a former student, Lorenz Mizler, it is said that he delayed his application so he would not be the thirteenth member of the society but the fourteenth. He had a fascination with numerology, and 14 belonged more to the B-A-C-H values than did 13. When he sat for his portrait, he had the artist paint a piece of music in his right hand, a canon triplex for six voices that was a musical puzzle.

Bach would be both baffled and pleased by the attention being given to him this year on the occasion of his 300th birthday. He would be awed by the way in which modern musicians have collected and recorded his works. And, this man who struggled for some identification and who coveted recognition and honor in his own day would weep for joy as he learned what his creative gifts have meant to generations who followed him.

As it so often happens with the world's greatest artists, Bach was almost forgotten during the first century following his death. Another well-known composer, Felix Mendelssohn-Bartholdy, is credited with the major resurrection of the Bach tradition, leading a performance of Bach's *St. Matthew Passion* 100 years after it was first heard in Leipzig.

Now during the 1985 Bach 300th anniversary year, dozens of major performances of *The Christmas Oratorio* have been scheduled. Some of them have been spread out as Bach intended, but many others have been marathon sessions of all six parts. Throughout the world, Bach enthusiasts have pulled out all the stops in scheduling tempting programs and appropriate celebrations.

Bach passed on his musical heritage as shown in this painting, *Sebastian Bach with His Family*, by Toby Edward Rosenthal.

In joining the *Mizler'sche Societät*, Bach also reached back to his childhood for the beloved tune from Luther that had echoed in his musical consciousness each Christmas season: *"Vom Himmel hoch da komm ich her."* He wrote out what he called "a few canonic variations of the Christmas hymn for the organ with two manuals and pedal" and submitted it as a qualifying work. They really were not variations but were rather a chorale fantasia in the form of contrapuntal embroideries on the hymn tune. It was his passage into the academy.

The weekly news magazine *Time* featured Bach as the subject of its cover story for its Christmas issue in 1968. Across the top of the cover painting by the late Ben Shahn was a banner bearing the legend, "Music from the Fifth Evangelist," picking up the term for Bach introduced by his famous biographer, Albert Schweitzer. Inside the magazine the article carried a headline that still applies wherever Bach is discovered these days:

A composer for all seasons—but especially for Christmas!

Psalm 98

Psalm 98
versification, Gracia Grindal, b. 1943

Heinrich Schütz, 1585-1672

Oh, sing a new song un - to God
God has made known his sav - ing pow'r
So make a joy - ful noise to God.
Now let the trum - pets praise the Lord

For the great won - der God has done.
Come to us in this ho - ly hour.
Sing, all the earth, with this new song,
And make a joy - ful noise to God!

Shout to our God, oh, sing God's praise,
The hills re - joice, the seas and flood
For un - to us our God is come!
Sing a new song, let joy in - crease,

For this great tri - umph of God's grace.
Shout with great joy that God is good.
Praise God with harp and sing a psalm.
Our Lord has come, the Prince of Peace!

Heinrich Schütz was one of the most celebrated composers of the seventeenth century, the first in a long line of German masters whose works dominated the musical scene up through the beginning of the twentieth century.

We mark Schütz's 400th birthday this year. Little is known about his life. He was born in Saxony. He studied in Kassel and in Venice with the Italian master, Giovanni Gabrieli, then served as kapellmeister to the Saxon court in Dresden most of his professional life. He made several visits to Copenhagen where he also served the royal court, and to Italy where he came to know the works of Monteverdi and other Italian masters of his time.

One of Schütz's important accomplishments was to bring characteristics of the Italian style into his music for the German church and court. His important works, mostly for voices and instruments, include settings of the *Resurrection History* and *The Seven Words on the Cross*. He was almost 80 years old when he wrote the *Christmas Oratorio*. Works such as these were to serve as models for several generations of composers down through the era of Bach and Handel.

"Psalm 98" is a simple hymnlike musical setting that appears in the *Becker Psalter*, which was first published in 1628. The words of the psalm were paraphrased in German by Cornelius Becker. The metrical structure allowed for the use, in each successive stanza, of the same hymnlike music.

In liturgical churches today Psalm 98 is one of the psalms appointed for Christmas Day. The English version of the metrical text appears here for the first time.

31

Break Forth, O Beauteous Heavenly Light

Johann Rist, 1606-1667
tr. John Troutbeck, 1832-1899

Johann Schop, 1600-1665
arr. J. S. Bach, 1685-1750

Break forth, O beau- teous heav'n- ly light, And
Ye shep- herds, shrink not with af- fright, But

ush- er in the morn- ing;
hear the an- gel's warn- ing.

This child now weak in in- fan- cy, Our

con- fi- dence and joy shall be, The

pow'r of Sa- tan break- ing, Our

peace e- ter- nal mak- ing.

Johann Sebastian Bach's most celebrated Christmas music is in the *Christmas Oratorio*, which he completed in 1734. This work recounts the story of Christmas in a set of six cantatas whose texts are drawn from the gospels of Luke and Matthew. Bach included nine chorale settings in the course of this extended work for chorus, soloists, and instruments. Two of the chorale settings are presented here in their basic four-voice structure for singing in parts or in unison with accompaniment.

"Break Forth, O Beauteous Heavenly Light" occurs in the second part of the oratorio, at the appearance of the angels to the shepherds. Bach used the second stanza of "All My Heart This Night Rejoices" to create a moment of contemplation, a brief contrast to the general mood of exultation that pervades the *Christmas Oratorio*.

32

Flute

Timpani

Bag Pipe

Bas Pommer

All My Heart This Night Rejoices

Paul Gerhardt, 1606-1676
tr. Catherine Winkworth, 1829-1878

Johann G. Ebeling, 1637-1676
arr. J. S. Bach, 1685-1750

1. All my heart this night re-joic-es,
2. Thee, dear Lord, with heed I'll cher-

es, As I hear, Far and
ish, Live to thee, And with

near, Sweet-est an-gel voic-
thee Dy-ing, shall not per-

es; "Christ is born!" their choirs are
ish; But shall dwell with thee for-

sing-ing, Till the air Ev-ery-where
ev-er, Far on high In the joy

Now with joy is ring-ing.
That can al-ter nev-er.

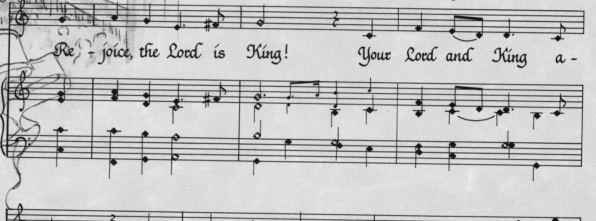

Rejoice, the Lord Is King

Charles Wesley, 1707-1788

George F. Handel, 1685-1759
arr. John Wilson, b. 1929

Re - joice, the Lord is King! Your Lord and King a -

dore; Mor - tals, give thanks and sing, And

tri - umph ev - er - more: Lift up your heart, lift

During the Bach Christmas chorales we kneel in adoration at the manger of the heavenly Child, Jesus the Redeemer. But George Frederick Handel's music incites us to stand, awed by the majestic presence of Christ the King, just as we have learned to do literally when we hear the opening strains of the "Hallelujah Chorus" from the *Messiah*.

The several famous Christmas hymns ascribed to Handel are all adaptations from larger works, oratorios and operas. He is known to have written only three hymn tunes, all of them around 1750 to words by Charles Wesley. We include one of them here, "Rejoice, the Lord Is King." This hymn, with its tune name Gopsal, is much better known in England than in America. It was written for solo or unison singing with keyboard accompaniment to be realized from a figured bass. The text shown here includes only the first stanza of Wesley's hymn.

34

35

Joy to the World

Isaac Watts, 1674 - 1748

attr. George F. Handel, 1685 - 1759
arr. Lowell Mason, 1792 - 1872

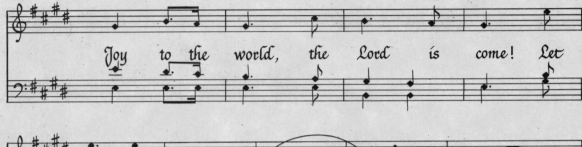

"Joy to the World" by Isaac Watts has become one of the most popular Christmas hymns in America. The words, like the text of Heinrich Schütz's Christmas psalm, are a paraphrase of Psalm 98.

The familiar melody, with the tune name Antioch, is usually identified as "arranged from Handel." The first phrase may be an adaptation of the jubilant "Glory to God" chorus in the *Messiah*; while the third phrase may derive from the tenor recitative, "Comfort Ye My People." But Handel would not be likely to recognize this well-known Christmas hymn as his own composition.

The musician credited with the adaptation from Handel is the nineteenth-century American, Lowell Mason (1792-1872). During Mason's time it was common to "compose" hymn tunes broadly derived from works of well-known European composers. The label "music made in America" supposedly did not carry great cultural prestige in its own right.

"Joy to the World" appears here in an early version from *Southern Harmony*, which incidentally, celebrates its 150th anniversary this year. The hymnal was first published in 1835. The arrangement here appeared in the 1854 edition of *Southern Harmony*, in a three-voiced texture with the "tune" in the middle voice.

36

A Masterpiece for Praise

JOHN FERGUSON

Try to imagine a festive Christmas worship without the inspiring sounds of a congregation led in carols and hymns by a fine pipe organ. Oh, yes, we have heard the story of "Silent Night"—the lovely Christmas hymn composed for guitar and voices because the organ broke down—but that is the exception which proves the rule. For centuries, the people of God have gathered in worship, led in their song by the organ.

Through these centuries many fine musicians have led from the organ bench as choirs and congregations sang their songs of praise. This year marks the 300th birthday of one of the greatest of these organists, Johann Sebastian Bach. His compositional genius has provided a rich treasury of music in almost every performing medium. But above all, it is his church music that is so precious, for it fuses an extraordinary musical ability with a fine theological sensitivity.

A great part of Bach's art is embodied in his organ music. Most authorities agree that his music for organ is the single greatest treasure in literature for the organ. Perhaps one reason for the brilliance of Bach's organ music is that he himself was a very fine organist. His reputation as a performer was so great that on at least one occasion another famed performer, André Raison, left town when he learned that he and Bach were to appear together!

Bach also put his knowledge of the organ to work as an organ consultant. He often was called to examine instruments and propose revisions or improvements. He also served as a kind of quality control expert, coming to a church to examine a new organ. With the leading citizens of the town and the organ builder in attendance, Bach would examine and play the new instrument to be sure that it was completed according to the terms of the contract between builder and client. These inspections were tense times for the builder as the legendary and knowledgeable organist made exceptional demands

upon the organ, usually in brilliant improvisations. Only after satisfying Bach's rigorous inspection would the town authorities agree to pay the organ builder for the work, which in large organs could represent well over a year of work. The dedication recital of today is but a weak remnant of what once was a very critical moment of truth for the completed organ and its builder.

What would Bach encounter if he were to visit an organ builder of today to examine their work? What would Bach notice as different if he were to visit a modern organ factory or shop, as most builders like to call their manufacturing facility? Before exploring this interesting

Photo: Pipe organ at University Baptist Church, Minneapolis, built by Lynn A. Dobson of Lake City, Iowa.

(upper left) The woodworker's skills are of utmost importance in organ building as ninety percent of an organ is constructed of wood. A carpenter is shown planing a section of the casing.

(left) A worker assembles the keys, which have been shaped from plumwood. Most organs have at least two keyboards.

(center top) Pipes are racked into a wind-chest. Each pipe must set perfectly so that no air leaks out at the foot. And the pipes must fit securely in their holes, so that they won't rattle or touch one another.

(center bottom) At Holtkamp Organ, pipes are made from an alloy of tin and lead in the traditional composition of fifty percent each. Molten metal is poured into a wooden trough, which is then "walked" down the length of the table, leaving a molten deposit. This hardens as it cools into a metal sheet, which is then cut and rolled to make pipes.

(upper right) Each pipe must be made to play or "voiced" and then adjusted or "finished" to sound its best in the final location.

(right) Rollers are assembled on the rollerboards, which is part of the mechanical action of an organ.

question, we will take a moment to look at the pipe organ and explain a few technical terms so that when we visit a shop with Bach we will better understand what is happening.

Simply stated, the organ is a large collection of whistles, some as small as pencils, others as long as 32 feet. Each whistle or pipe is made to play (voiced), usually in the organ builder's shop, and then adjusted (finished) to sound its best in its final location. Pipes are arranged in rows (ranks) of like-sounding pipes with one rank for each key. The rank is made to play by a control called a stop. (In early organs all the pipes controlled by a single key sounded whenever the key was depressed. An early improvement was the stop, which silenced or stopped selected pipes of the many controlled by one key.) In addition to a family name (principal, gedackt, trompette, etc.), each stop is usually given a pitch length, e.g., 16',

8', 4', 2'. This designation in feet refers to the approximate length required for an open pipe to sound the lowest key on the manual or pedal keyboard. For example, an 8' principal stop would require an open pipe about 8' tall for the lowest key of the keyboard. When playing middle C on the manual with an 8' stop, the pitch is the same as middle C on the piano; the 4' stop would sound one octave higher, and the 2' stop would sound two octaves higher. Conversely, the 16' stop sounds one octave below the 8' stop.

As implied in the above discussion, each organ key controls many individual pipes depending upon the stops selected by the organist. This aspect of the organ makes it different from other instruments; the organist has available many individual sound sources (the pipes) and combines them to create rich ensemble sonorities.

The heart of the pipe organ is the wind-chest upon

which the pipes stand. Here wind is admitted into the pipes by opening and closing valves placed inside the wind-chest. Organ builders use more than one system for opening a valve to allow a pipe or pipes to sound. The oldest and still the best method, the one Bach knew, involves a direct mechanical linkage from keyboard to pipes. This method is called mechanical or, more specifically, tracker action, named after the tracker, which is one of the parts of a typical mechanical action. Other more recent types of key action use electricity or a combination of electric and pneumatic action to open the valves. (An electric action should not be confused with instruments whose sound source is electric or electronic.)

Wind to blow the pipes is stored in boxes called reservoirs so that the organist's need for air to supply many or few pipes may be met with a stable supply of wind. Today an electric blower usually supplies the wind, making instruments much more stable than many of the organs of Bach's time. (One wit has speculated that a pragmatic reason for Bach's many children was the need for a steady supply of organ pumpers!)

While simple in basic concept, most organs have at least two keyboards (manuals) and a pedalboard controlling many pipes. Larger instruments can be remarkably complex because of the multimanuals controlling many ranks of pipes.

Now back to our question. What would Bach say if he were to drop in on a typical organ shop of today? More than anything else, he would be sure to observe that organ building is more like organ building of his day than it is different. It is still a craft requiring skilled workers who produce essentially custom-made products designed and built for a specific location and situation. Today, as in Bach's time, most of the work is done by hand with few labor-saving shortcuts.

Most organ shops are still relatively small operations employing from three to fifteen skilled workers and producing from two to eight instruments per year. Many are old family firms. An example is the Holtkamp Organ Company in Cleveland where the third generation of Holtkamps are in charge of a business that dates from 1855. Such a family business would remind Bach of the famous families of organ builders of his time.

An interesting development in the last 20 years has been the emergence of new, small firms usually founded by one person interested in organ building who, with the help of one or two associates, begins to produce small instruments. One such firm is that of John Brombaugh, originally located in Ohio but now relocated in Oregon. Another is Lynn Dobson of Iowa. From very modest beginnings, these builders have developed fine reputations for quality instruments while remaining essentially small in size.

Firms like these would not surprise Bach, but he would be dumbfounded by a company like Schantz in Orville, Ohio. While it, too, is a family business, now controlled by a fourth generation of the Schantz family, the company has grown to be a very large business. Founded in 1873, it now employs over 85 workers and produces from 20 to 30 organs a year. One reason that Schantz is so large is that it is one of the few firms that makes almost everything that goes into the organ from blower to pipes, although even Schantz relies upon a special supplier for its keyboards.

As in Bach's time, pipe organ builders are a conservative lot. Change comes about slowly, if at all. This is especially evident in the pipe shop where the many sizes and shapes of pipes are produced just like they were in Bach's day. While some have experimented with materials like aluminum, most continue to favor an alloy of lead and tin when making the metal pipes. Many builders do not have a shop large enough to make their own pipes, so they order them from one of the organ supply houses here or in Europe. Those that do make pipes tend to do the whole thing, casting the metal in a long, shallow box just like one Bach would recognize. Since various pipes are made with different percentages of lead and tin in varying thicknesses of metal, it is helpful to do the casting in the pipe shop, thus reducing the need for a large inventory of sheets (rolls) of pipe metal.

The rolls of metal await to be cut to patterns, shaped over mandrels, and soldered, resulting in the pipes we see. Aside from the electric soldering iron, a pipemaker of 1700 would feel right at home in a pipe shop of today; so little has changed.

Some pipes are made of copper and some of wood, as has been true for centuries. The names of the various stops haven't changed much either. The principal—an open metal stop of rich, robust sound—is still the backbone of the organ. Flute and reed stops, many named

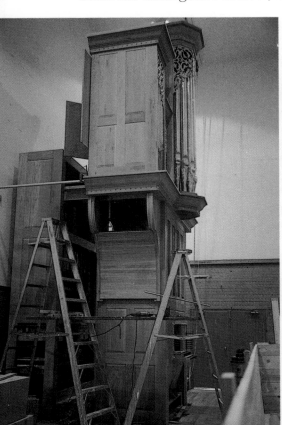

(left) An organ is set up in the erecting room before installation in a church.
(center) A worker leathers the bellows, which blows air into the wind-chest.
(right) The rollerboard links the action of the keyboard to the pipes. The vertical wooden slats, called "trackers," distinguish a "tracker organ."

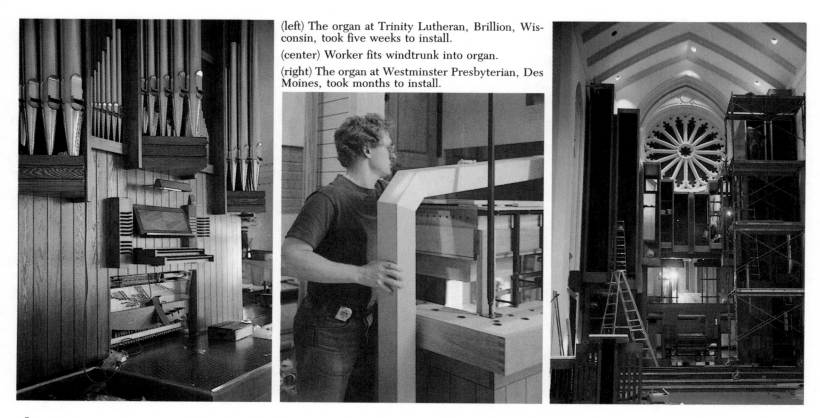

(left) The organ at Trinity Lutheran, Brillion, Wisconsin, took five weeks to install.

(center) Worker fits windtrunk into organ.

(right) The organ at Westminster Presbyterian, Des Moines, took months to install.

after instruments common in Bach's day, complete the tonal palette of the builder.

Once made, the pipes are taken to a voicing room where a skilled artisan makes the pipes sing. Voicing is crucially important for good organ building. Many minute adjustments can be made to a pipe in the process of giving it voice. The tonal quality, the unique personality, of one builder's organ is determined to a great extent in the work of the voicer. This art has changed little over the years, although various styles of voicing go in and out of favor. A voicer's tools from 1700 would not be a mystery to the voicer of today.

Wind-chests, especially those for tracker action instruments, are little changed in basic design from those of Bach's time. Wood is still the primary material, although some modern materials (Teflon for one) have replaced natural materials for some parts of a chest. Because so much of an organ is of wood (wind-chests, reservoirs, sometimes even the pipes carrying the wind from blower to reservoir to chest), an organ shop is a place where much woodworking is done. While some modern machines make the woodworking a bit faster and easier, the basic processes are much the same. The smell of glue and wooden pegs are still very much a part of the environment of most organ shops.

The two parts of the organ most changed through the centuries are the blower and console. An adequate wind supply was a great challenge for the 18th century builder. While a few organs did use water power to pump the bellows, most relied upon human organ pumpers. Some authorities have speculated that perhaps Bach's famous Toccata in D Minor might have been improvised for one of his examinations of a new organ. The low pedal note with the huge chord building up above makes a terrific demand upon the wind supply, which must have caused many an 18th century builder to pale, and pumper to work furiously! Today Bach could include chords as large and long lasting as he would ever want; the electric blower would be more than adequate. In fact, some contemporary builders believe that our modern organs have too

stable and ample a wind supply, so they deliberately engineer a bit of "wobble" into the wind supply so that the organs of today behave more like those of Bach's day.

Bach, famous for his creativity in using the tonal resources of the organ, also would be very interested in the console of many organs built today. It is now possible to provide a memory system whereby the organist can preselect certain combinations of stops and activate them by the push of a button, achieving much more radical and quick changes of tonal color than Bach ever could have achieved. Many modern American consoles, using electricity to move small stop controls up and down or in and out, would be a surprise for someone used to large stop knobs which had to be pulled out by hand, often with the help of assistants.

The question is still before us. How would Bach react to organ building as practiced today? Probably he would observe that it is more like what he experienced in the 18th century than different—an amazing statement considering the many technological changes that have so influenced our life-style in the second half of this century. One can be sure that Bach would ask to play and hear some of America's finest instruments because the answer to the question finally depends upon the resulting sound. My guess is that if he were to play some of these instruments, for example the magnificent Fisk organ in the House of Hope Presbyterian Church, St. Paul, Minnesota, he would be as delighted and impressed as he was with any of the organs he examined in his time.

Great organ building of today, as in Bach's day, is still a craft; each instrument produced is unique, designed by the builder for a specific location. This design is then realized by a small crew of skilled workers who use methods steeped in tradition to give voice to a machine of wood and metal. When the psalmist sings, "Let everything that has breath praise the Lord," the organ is included. It, too, is a symbol of God's marvelous creation—an instrument made from things in the creation, given voice by skilled artisans, and utilized to sing in praise of Father, Son, and Holy Spirit.

MELODIES of a CHRISTMAS

not so long ago

A Picture Story by Eric Hanson

Come the first of December Christmas music begins to edge out the songs of the "Top 40" on the Radio.

Sleigh bells ring ~ are ya' listenin'?

On T.V., everybody from Perry Como to the Muppets hosts their own holiday special.

And each favorite Christmas song and carol brings with it cherished memories of Christmases gone by.

1955? It hardly seems possible!

That's your Dad!

where

Photo Album

WHITE CHRISTMAS IRVING BERLIN

Oh there's no place like home for the Holidays!

To those who never tire of those old, familiar Christmas songs (and those not-so-olden days) we dedicate these pages.

E.H.

NORMAN LUBOFF CHOIR

The Christmas season at home always began in Mom's kitchen as the smell of baking spritz (and the sound of Mom's singing) filled the house.

♪ Nar Julesmorgen glimmar ♪

the Juleneg

Dad in his Workshop

SUGAR

The birds' Christmas was full of song and chatter

There were other things hidden in the upstairs closet too!

Sooner or later (usually sooner) the Christmas records were brought down from the upstairs closet to be played over and over and over!

Don't peek!

CHRISTMAS IN SCANDINAVIA
AXEL STORDAHL
PERRY COMO

WINTER WONDERLAND

The Ray Charles Singers

note the ears

BING CROSBY

CHRISTMAS

George Greeley at the piano

The NUTCRACKER SUITE performed by LEOPOLD STOKOWSKI and his orchestra

(the records were red vinyl!)

"If I hear "Jingle Bells" one more time I think I'll scream!"

Away in a Manger" (Lisa's favorite carol)

JINGLE BELLS! JINGLE BELLS

EH

At school everyone practiced carols for the **Christmas** pageant and made **Christmas** decorations for the classroom.

Paper Snowflakes

Paper Chains

The big night came a week before **Christmas**,

Si-i-lent Night!

Ho-o-ly Night!

MRS. ROREM SECOND GRADE

they sound like angels!

Up on the housetop reindeer paws

Sing nicely

Our teacher in the wings

There were still special gifts to be made.

uh...um...

Tommy, who forgot his lines.

Pa-rum-pa-pum pum!

I thought this was the best pageant ever!

Trivet made from milk bottle caps

Paperweight for Dad's desk

We wish you a merry Christmas

Caroling up to the 5th & 6th grade classrooms.

Suddenly it was only a couple of days before **Christmas**.

GRYGLA BANK

DECEMBER
S M T W T F S

EH

Finally, it was Christmas Eve!

Mother's busy month of preparation was nearly over!

O Tannenbaum! O Tannenbaum!

Joy to the world!

The last present wrapped

The tree, fresh from the Y's Men's lot, had been up for a week.

The familiar carols made Christmas Eve services much easier for a kid to sit through.

Some of Mother's relatives came for Christmas Eve —

Uncle Seth "dreaming of a white Christmas"

Glo-o-oo-ooo-ooo-Ria! In Excelsis Deo!

The children's choir sang sweetly.

I'll be home for Christmas" meant driving an hour and a half to Gran'ma & Gran'pa's house.

Over the River and Through the Wood" on the old Northwest Highway.

And "Oh, for the Christmas Pie!"

Peace on Earth Good Will to All

MELVA ROREM

I walk from my mailbox with a glad heart, holding in my hand Christmas greetings from Alaska to Florida, from New York to California, from Scotland, Germany, Denmark, and Africa. I am one of the nearly three billion Americans receiving Christmas cards during this joyous season. Footsore mail carriers deliver an average of over 75 cards to every United States family. To mail these cards takes over 60 million dollars worth of stamps, over one-fifth of the government's entire postal revenue.

In earlier days, Christians of Russia greeted each other on Christmas morn with the words "Christ is born!" The reply, "He is indeed," was given with an embrace and a

A 1980s reproduction by Hallmark Cards of the first known Christmas card.

kiss. The celebration of the birth of Christ continues to draw from our hearts warm greetings. And when we cannot see our friends, we send a Christmas card that proclaims our friendship and good wishes for another year. Indeed, the annual exchange of Christmas cards sometimes is the only connection maintained by two people.

Greetings of various kinds have been exchanged for centuries. Hundreds of years before the pharaohs of Egypt, runners sent greetings from one ruler to another. Sometimes the greetings were verbal; at other times they were inscribed on cylinders of clay. These cylinders had outer jackets of clay that served as envelopes. The receiver simply knocked the jacket off with a small chisel and hammer. Sometimes the greetings were accompanied by a substantial gift such as an elegant handicraft or, perhaps, a group of servants. As long as gifts have been sent, greetings also have been sent.

In Christian times gift giving was common. At festive times in Rome, gifts were exchanged. Christians then, as now, gave gifts to God through the church and to each other.

The first written Christmas greetings were elaborately decorated letterheads. Writing masters, who wished to show parents the progress of their children, had them decorate sheets of paper with birds, scrolls, and other intricate penmanship exercises, with a Christmas greeting written below.

Most historians agree that an Englishman, Sir Henry Cole, was the first person to have a Christmas card designed. He was busier than usual just before Christmas 1846. In other years he had written Christmas letters to relatives and friends, but this year he realized he would not have time. So he decided to send a decorated Christmas card to all his relatives and friends.

He commissioned an artist-friend from the Royal Academy, John Calcott Housley, to carry out the idea. Housley designed a three-paneled card with a trellis entwined with a grapevine. The largest panel showed a family Christmas party. The panels on either side depicted two of the oldest Christmas customs—feeding the hungry and clothing the needy. The words of greeting have lasted through the years: "A Merry Christmas and a Happy New Year to you."

During the next few years Christmas cards were sold at stationery stores only rarely. More often they were printed as orders for individuals. In 1862, some cards were printed for general use in England; sales picked up when Charles Goodall and Sons issued a series of cards. After 1871, when Raphael Tuck bought and published original verses from poets and postage rates dropped, the sending of Christmas cards became a general practice.

In these early days artwork by the best artists and verses by the best poets were purchased for use on Christmas cards. As poet laureate of England, Lord Tennyson rejected an offer to write a dozen poems to be used for cards. Later, however, he accepted an offer for 1000 guineas to write verses for cards. This may have been more than he was paid for any literary work. Artists from the Royal Academy were commissioned to produce series of cards. In 1882, one firm paid artists $35,000 for original drawings; while in 1874 a collection of paintings was sold for $10,000 to the Foster Company.

In 1867 the Marcus Ward Company began to publish

cards. Their cards reached the highest level of excellence. Prize competitions were held and the highest prize, 250 pounds, was awarded to Alice Havers for her painting, "A Dream of Patience." Soon staff writers and artists were hired. Ward's famous series of four cards on the Nativity were lithographed in gold and other colors.

At the same time, printers in Germany began printing exquisite chromos, very delicately blended lithographed colors that appeared to be oil paintings. The chromos were imported by card companies and mounted on cards with decorated borders.

Louis Prang, who originated the idea of the Christmas card in America, is known as "the father of the American Christmas card." Once a skilled printer living in Breslau, Germany, he became a penniless outcast during the German revolution of 1848. So he sailed for America, arriving in New York on April 5, 1850. From there he went to Roxbury, a suburb of Boston, where he set up a printing shop. Before Prang, Christmas cards had been imported from England and other European countries. But the Christmas card tradition really did not become established here until it ceased to be a European product with the limitations this necessarily involved. Prang's plant in Roxbury and his production of cards designed and printed in America not only established a line of trade that grew into a tremendous American greeting card industry, but also led to the creation of a market and an extension of the custom on such a worldwide scale that it can be described as a universal holiday phenomenon.

During 10 years of hard work and much experimenting both in areas of production techniques and of marketing, Prang succeeded in perfecting a process of lithographic color printing, usually from eight but sometimes from as many as 20 plates, which gained for him the admiration of experts on both sides of the Atlantic. He originated the first open competition for Christmas card designs in 1880, offering substantial prizes to winning designers. Prang's enterprise and mode in projecting and merchandising methods were remarkable and had an immediate effect on his chief competitors and leading publishers in England.

At the beginning, the Prang cards were small, simple cards (3½ by 2 inches or 4 by 2½ inches) printed on one side of the card only. Flowers, birds, or flowers and birds grouped together brought greetings of couplets or prose, usually fairly brief, but varied to suit every need.

One of the novelties that swept into vogue, lasting for several years on both sides of the Atlantic, was the black background cards. The contrast made the bright colors and contours of the emblems, scrolls, flowers, or bird designs stand out brilliantly from the solid black background. Red backgrounds also were used, giving a more festive gaiety to the cards than the black backgrounds.

(top left) A beribboned nativity scene printed by Mobrays of England.

(bottom left) Red fringe and tassels adorn this card from the 1880s, which opens to reveal another snow scene.

(right) Prize-winning card design by Lizbeth Humphrey was printed in 1882 by Louis Prang and Company.

An early Louis Prang Christmas card with holly and mistletoe decorations was a long card 3½ by 8¼ inches in size with a rich, red background. The design consisted of a sepia monochrome drawing of six children of various ages, with two white doves each with a blue streamer waving from his neck with the inscriptions "Joy" and "Mirth" on them. The whole was enclosed in a frame of holly leaves and berries and one or two sprigs of mistletoe. The greeting that appeared on a white panel beneath the picture consisted of six lines which emphasized the sentiment of the card:

Ho, for the merry, merry Christmas time,
With its feast and fun, and the pantomime.
When good humor reigns, and a gay content
Is boon companion in all merriment.
Such a Christmas bright, with its frolic joys
Belongs to all good little girls and boys.

Sometimes cards with the sharp-thorned holly leaves and the blood-red berries had serious verses and were associated in the minds of the devout with the suffering and blood of Christ. They gave to holly a certain religious significance, making it still more suitable for Christmas.

Prang's cards had been enlarged to 5½ by 2¾ inches and 6¾ by 2½ inches by the 1870s. Also, decorations began to appear on the reverse side of the card and the name of the designer of the card began to be included. Prang refused to print trick or mechanical cards, which had become popular. To him the Christmas card remained a *card*, embellished by pictorial design and lettering and each one more beautiful than the one before. He employed fine artists. Their technical excellence and their perfect finish as chromolithographs hardly ever faltered, making them special finds for the collector. Prang card collections can be seen in the Boston Library and in the Christmas card collection at the Museum of New York.

Prang died on June 14, 1909. He was irritated in the 1890s by the cheap and gaudy cards that were being printed. In his prime, he printed over five million Christmas cards a year.

For a few years after the turn of the century, cards became cheap novelties. Every type of illustration was used except the true Christmas symbols. Picture postcards forced the Christmas card into the same format. Fad after fad took over in America, and a huge number of cards were sent during this period. In 1913 a sensational giftcard was introduced: a 16 inch phonograph record with the tune of "Auld Lang Syne." A baritone sang these words:

Across the years on Christmas Day
    Amid the Christmas cheer,
I'm sending thee a greeting gay
    And wishes most sincere.

Chorus
May every hour bring thee joy,
   All happiness be thine.
And merriment and sweet content
   Bless all thy Christmas time.
And when the Christmas Day is o'er
   My wish I still repeat—
May each tomorrow bring a store
   Of gladness true and deep.

Chorus
Of gladness true and deep and strong,
   Of pleasures fine and free,
So may the coming year be rich
   In happiness to thee.

During World War I many cards were printed for "the boys over there." Verses were written especially for them. Families and friends had been forcibly dispersed. People often had to spend Christmas in circumstances that contrasted sharply with memories of past Christmases. The number of absent friends was greater than ever before. But even in the grimmest years of the great struggle, illustrations and texts concentrated on the sentimental and peaceful recollections of Christmas past or looked forward to similar circumstances in the future. The enemy and the blood and sweat of the life and death struggle were ignored in the majority of cards in much the same way as they were ignored in the songs of war.

The used-card fad also developed in the early 1900s out of necessity. Every card was expensive compared to those of today. An embellished, silk-fringed, deluxe card usually cost $3.00. Cards for a score of friends would cost too much, and social snobbery kept people from buying cheaper cards.

The problem was solved in this way. Senders simply wrote their names beneath the original signatures and then sent the secondhand cards. In England where the custom was strongest, a firm rose to the occasion by supplying used cards. Kriskards, Ltd., employed a clerical staff to sign the cards with names from telephone directories. Sometimes famous people were hired to sign their names to batches of cards. To complete the process the cards were sent to the "soiling department" where smudges and creases were provided so that no one would know they were new cards.

One of the characteristics of early Christmas cards was its recurring interest in children as prominent motifs of design. The large families and the tradition that brought them together for a Christmas celebration naturally laid an emphasis on children at this season.

Washington Irving wrote:

It is a beautiful arrangement, derived from days of yore, that the festival, which commemorates the announcement of the religion of peace and love, has been made the season for gathering together of family connections, and drawing closer again those bands of kindred hearts, which the cares and pleasures and sorrows of the world are continually operating to cast loose: of calling back the children of the family who have launched forth in life and wandered widely asunder, once more to assemble about the paternal hearth, that rallying place of affections, there to grow young and loving again, among the endearing memories of childhood.

(left) Postcards printed in Germany flooded the market in the early 1900s.

(right) The tradition of sending Christmas cards encircles the world as evidenced by this Chinese card with an embroidered design.

Old woodcuts and engravings, the forerunner of the Christmas card as we know it, regularly concentrated on the figure of the infant Christ. His blessing was asked to make the New Year peaceful, happy, and prosperous. These old presentations of the lightly draped baby and child figures, although they were representative of the child Jesus, were definitely religious in significance and devotional in appearance and may be taken as forerunners of the child motif on Christmas cards. They emphasized the purity and innocence of children in a way that indicates the chief significance of the incarnation, 2000 years ago.

Often entire family parties were pictured—not just children alone. Photographs of family groups are often used as Christmas greetings today, and the stiff and formal groupings previously used have, thanks to modern photography, relaxed.

In the early 1900s, cards sometimes pictured customs of the homelands of the immigrants. Scandinavians in this country sent postcards that pictured feeding the birds at Christmastime. Another custom that was shown was children knocking at a friend's door bringing the gift of a festive bouquet of flowers.

The Hallmark Company in Kansas City, Missouri, is the largest greeting card industry in our country today, printing 10 million cards a day. Hallmark serves 100 countries and employs 17 languages. Their creative staff of 600 is the largest in the world.

Joyce C. Hall, founder of Hallmark Cards, Inc., was born August 29, 1891 in David City, Nebraska. He had little formal education and came from a poor family, but this did not prevent him from heading one of this country's greatest industries. He was the friend of two presidents and a prime minister, a patron of the arts, and a recipient of high honors from three countries.

Although he became a wealthy man, wealth was never foremost in his mind. In his autobiography, *When You Care Enough*, he wrote: "If a man goes into business with the idea of making a lot of money, chances are he won't. But if he puts service and quality first, the money will take care of itself. Producing a first-class product that is a real need is a much stronger motivation than getting rich."

He ruled employees as a benevolent patriarch—advising, cajoling, reprimanding, always helping out if misfortune struck. As a result, his workers showered their "Mr. J. C." with warmth just short of adulation. He *was* Hallmark Cards for 56 years. In 1966 he stepped aside as chief executive officer and his son, Donald J. Hall, took over. He continued, however, as chairman of the board and kept a close watch on quality, until his death in 1982. Donald Hall continues in his father's footsteps. Today at Christmastime, Hallmark cards touch every continent, their messages ranging from comic hilarity to devout messages of Christmas peace and goodwill.

Recently a friend asked me, "Why is it that during the busiest season of the year we take time to write letters that are sent along with Christmas cards to all our friends and relatives?" I suspect it is because the letters and cards are symbols of friendship, cementing relationships for another year. And like the Russians of old we delight to share the good news of this joyous season, "Christ is born!"

(top left) Artist S. Granitsch portrays a tender moment on this Swiss card.
(bottom left) Bright colors stand out against black on this 1928 card.
(right) Classical artistry marks this Italian card.

Township Christmas

JUSTIN ISHERWOOD

Winter brings an armistice to the countryside. The fields lie frozen, resting from the marathon event of summer just run with the sun. A peaceful product grows now from the land.

Christmas is a farmer's holiday. The reason is one of logistics. Memorial Day, Fourth of July, Labor Day all come in the green season, at a time when farmers cannot take liberties with their vocation. That the nation does celebrate with mass exodus, all the cars packed and outward-bound to some haven, makes little difference.

Christmas comes at a time when work has cooled its fevered pace; the mows, granaries, and warehouses attest to the fulfillment of spring, summer, and harvest. The great work is finished.

Christmas has a primitive heritage. Sky watchers, who by nature were farmers, have for millenia noted the autumnal declination of the sun, noted the days becoming both

A peaceful product grows now from the land.

shorter and colder. Because they had a direct relationship with the earth, this no doubt caused a reverberate fear the sun would sink altogether beneath the horizon, never to rise again.

Perhaps their celestial instrument

was a tree seen from their habitation, perhaps a large rock. One day, two-thirds of the way through December, notice was given the sun would rise high again. This observation of the sun rising on the north side of the tree assured the farmer of the return of the sun and its connected growing season.

Modern farmers are yet tied to such ancient solar rites; some small muscle twitches at solstice. A near universal time of celebration, feast days, dances, and gift giving, its importance is held within our blood as an almost genetic response to a tilted planet's return swing about a nearby star.

Winter always provokes the struggle to survive. We have little difficulty in understanding why this is so, with blizzards and the worst cold yet to be told. The fall rush of canning, pickling, and hunting is but preparation to endure winter's coming, to survive to a distant spring.

Christmas is a time that makes us believers in magic. We as a people are so touched by the season that the selfish find themselves generous and the quiet find themselves singing.

It is a time when people become a little crazy, a time when normal people take to hiding things in secret places. It is a time when country children sneak to the barn on Christmas Eve to wait in the dark so that they might hear cows speak in human tongues.

It is a time when the weed pullers of summer walk their fields spreading thistle, sunflower, and rye seeds to gain the blessed flight of birds over their land, in belief that feathered prayers are best.

That the season is generous cannot be doubted. Cash register carols ring in the ears of the nation's GNP. While we have gained with invention a multitude of curiosities, we have lost something of self-expression, a quality thought quaint. Yet, it is personal expression that reinforces the bonds of friends and family

and that repairs the rents made in the communal fabric. Its quality is one of goodness. For those having a generous solid character; what is put in will also flow out. Gifts make people as sure as people make gifts.

Remembered are all the knitted socks, caps, and mittens that mothers forced habitually on children, despite their best efforts to lose, mutilate, or outgrow them. Somehow mothers embodied good health in

Christmas is a time that makes us believers in magic.

their children by the sheer number of such articles they could produce.

Flannel pajamas and quilts stuffed with raw wool or old wedding suits gave warm comfort in wood-heated, sawdust-insulated houses, which held pitifully little heat by morning.

Indeed, there were store-bought BB guns and toy trains that puffed flour smoke. There were Raggedy Ann dolls, and bicycles, and light-bulb ovens, and baseball bats, and Flexible Flyers, and ice skates and, and, and—and all so child necessary. Beyond store-bought things were those contraptions, those inventions of glue and jack plane, alchemies of countersunk screw and dovetail mortise. They were gifts of the sort remembered, which gave off an affection if only from the lingering warmth of their manufacture. The spokeshave conveyed the heat of the builder into the wood grain. It was caught there, enmeshed in the fiber and net of a tree's core, only to be released slowly, the effect left to ripple across generations. There were dollhouses with tiny doors and itsy-bitsy cupboards. There were bookshelves and basswood mixing spoons, breadboards and spice racks. A coffee table with purple blemishes testified to the fence staples some great grandfather had driven into the tree, the iron taken till all that remained was the tinted tattle of wood. There was a child's wagon with lathe-turned white ash wheels. The basement oozed to the rest of the house the aroma of woodworking. A cradle with birch headboard and rockers cut from wind-shaped limbs, a dulcimer of prized black walnut, a four-horse team with bobsled whittled from a block of white pine all took form there. Patient fingers made little ears and whittled almost breathing nostrils. The leather harness had all the lines; and the ironbound bobs were connected beneath by tiny iron rods so the bobs would swing opposite, just like the real bobsleds that hauled away the great trees of the once near wilderness. A gift of the early days, it ties together all the years. And a rocking chair—made from homegrown pine, pegged, and glued—lulled to sleep three generations of babies and rocked away the anxious days of two world wars and one jungle fight.

There were simpler gifts of a pancake breakfast taken to neighbors, or the sudden appearance of two full cords of oak firewood, or snowtires

A gift of the early days, it ties together all the years.

mysteriously installed. Notes found in the bottom of stockings promised two Sunday afternoons of ice-skating adventures or three Saturday mornings without chores to go romp the woods. Other simple notes promised to show a favorite fishing hole or a tree where flickers nested.

There was gift in all the cookies made and cut in the shape of angels, stars, and deer that flew. A haunting gift of powerful pride was given children, that they might decorate stars from the humble perch of a country kitchen, cloistered behind its steamed-up windows.

The season was popcorn, grown in the garden and wildly crossed with Indian corn to produce among the bright yellow kernels spotted ones of red and purple. Shelled on the living room floor, the cobs were tossed to the fire. Hazelnuts were just for kids sitting cross-legged to crack. Ice skating on the irrigation pit meant popple branch hockey sticks and granite stone pucks. Hot cider, suet pudding, black fudge, cranberry bread, popcorn balls, and oyster suppers punctuated the season.

And the great green tree brought home from the woodlot in the emptied honey wagon swelled the whole house with its vapors. Its fragrance and good cheer left few lives untouched.

Christmas in the township catches hold of the generosity first given by the land. It is a season that knows what a good gift is, one that keeps on giving, echoing down what hard walls time makes. It was in just such a country place that angels were heard to sing of a child lain in a feedbox. It was, as all farmers know, a good place to be born and a good place for a promise to begin.

The Happiest of Times

ANNE COCHRAN

I took down the Indian corn today and hung the balsam wreath. I am very sentimental at holiday times, perhaps because they were such times of warmth and happiness in my home when I was a child. We were like the Cratchits in those depression days, living simply but rich in love for each other. Christmas was a joyous time of giving and receiving.

The Michigan landscape, masked in winter's gown of snow, was like all the Christmas cards. The snow covered the dreariness of the barren winter landscape; abandoned farm machinery and tumbled buildings became objects of white sculpture.

We had many traditions, and oyster stew on Christmas Eve was one of them. Christmas Day saw us, after our family gift giving, off to one grandmother's home for dinner with all the aunts and uncles and cousins, and on to another grandmother's home for a cold supper with the other aunts and uncles and cousins. At every point there was an exchange of presents so by the time we stumbled out of the car at midnight, drowsy from our sleepy ride home, we had none of the letdown that usually comes on Christmas. We were surfeited with gifts picked with just us in mind (Louisa Mae Alcott books, Monopoly games, etc.) and all the love that went with them. The radios and videogames found under today's trees can never replace the oranges and tangerines that looked like golden balls and seemed to have the exotic mystery of frankincense.

I can still recall the smell of my grandfather's cigar as he thumped and grumped with the "grown-ups" while we sat in the "other parlor" and played Authors or Who-Got-What with our cousins. At the first stop, my paternal grandmother set a table gleaming with cut glass and fine china. After dinner the women gathered in the kitchen, laughing and chatting as they washed and dried the plates back to shining perfection.

At the other grandparents in the country, we pulled the sleds out of the barn. Even the aunts and uncles went sledding, until twilight stilled the scene. It was the happiest of times. In my child's eye I pictured the year as an obelisk with Christmas at the top and the rest of the year as a climb to the peak.

It was a simpler time. It was the happiest of times.

England

Twelve Days of Celebration

Christmas in the British Isles

LA VERN J. RIPPLEY

The most recognized sign of a British Christmas is the evergreen tree amply decorated, gayly lighted, and supported at the root by colorful toys and gifts. Even today, the 1850 word-picture drawn by Charles Dickens in *A Christmas Tree* remains valid:

I have been looking on this evening at a merry company of children assembled round that pretty German toy, a Christmas tree. . . . It was brilliantly lighted by a multitude of little tapers; and everywhere sparkled and glittered with bright objects. There were rosy-cheeked dolls hiding behind green leaves and real watches (with moveable hands, at least, and an endless capacity for being wound up) dangling from innumerable twigs; there were French polished tables, chairs, bedsteads, eight-day clocks, and various other articles of domestic furniture (wonderfully made in tin) perched among the boughs, as if in preparation for some fairy housekeeping; there were jolly, broad-faced little men, much more agreeable in appearance than many real men—and no wonder, for their heads took off and showed them to be full of sugarplums; there were fiddles and drums, tambourines, books, work boxes, paint boxes, trinkets for the elder girls, far brighter than any grown-up gold and jewels; and there were guns, swords, and banners, witches standing in enchanted rings of pasteboard to tell fortunes; there were teetotums, humming pots, needle cases, pen wipers, smelling bottles, conversation cards, bouquet holders, real fruit . . . in short, there was everything and more!

Festooning the tree has long been the duty of parents: strings of beads, tiny flags, stars and shields of gilt paper, as well as lace bags filled with candies decorate most trees. So do ornaments and presents—dolls, toy carts with horses, and plenty of brightly colored ribbon. In times past, only after the candles were lighted on Christmas Eve or Christmas morning were the children allowed to rush into the room in order to add their own paper chains, stars, hearts, or fairy figures to the beauty of the tree.

The "German toy," as Dickens called it, may have reached England earlier than the 1840s, but it was Prince Albert and Queen Victoria who popularized it by including a tree decorated with candles, tinsel, and ornaments according to the German custom in their Christmas celebration of 1841. The 1864 *Book of Days* carried the following remark: "Within the last 20 years and apparently since the marriage of Queen Victoria with Prince Albert, previous to which time it was almost unknown in this country, the custom has been introduced to England with the greatest success." In succeeding years a huge Christmas tree was usually set up on the site of the 1851 Great Exhibition (which also was Prince Albert's creation). Today, no London Christmas is complete without a visit to Trafalgar Square, which annually, since 1946, boasts a large Christmas tree donated by the people of Oslo, Norway, in gratitude for the British role in Norway's regaining independence from Nazi occupation. At the opposite end of Trafalgar Square is located St. Paul's Cathedral, to which the queen gives two Christmas trees. One stands lighted outside the cathedral, while the other becomes the focal point inside. Here people leave presents for children and needy adults.

Today's custom of a Christmas tree replaced an old English custom, the kissing bough. The kissing bough was a double hoop covered with greenery, candles, apples, small gifts, and ornaments that was hung from the ceiling in a notable spot in every cottage.

Both customs are of pagan origin, yet have persisted long after the Christian religion replaced paganism. Christianity came early to the British Isles, more than a millennium before the Christmas tree, by way of the Romans who arrived around 50 A.D. and stayed until about 400 A.D. Long before the Germanic evergreen made its triumphal entry under Prince Albert, Germanic tribes of Anglos, Saxons, and Jutes roamed the British Isles almost at will. Today only the misty legends of such figures as King Arthur hint of the struggle the British inhabitants waged against their fifth and sixth century usurpers. In the process, the Roman plantations and both the Celtic and the Latin languages vanished for the most part. Only Welsh Christianity and the Celtic Welsh language (which is still mandatory in the primary schools of Wales) held out in the beleaguered but impregnable mountain fortresses along the western seaboard. England in the main became Anglo-Saxon. England sank under the rule of a Heptarchy, the seven kingdoms of Kent, Wessex, Sussex, East Anglia, Mercia, and Northumbria—all of which constantly squabbled, built, dissolved, and shifted alliances (as well as frontiers) and left a savage, shapeless, and tangled history.

The one bright light in these dark ages was the missionary zeal of St. Augustine from Rome and of St. Columba and St. Aidan from Ireland. Along about 600 A.D., they sufficiently impressed local kinglets to accept Christianity and to forcibly convert their subjects. Gradually, as Christianity took root, the Saxon kingdoms united under Egbert of Wessex, who in 827 brought the other six kingdoms under his rule. From this Egbert, the present Queen Elizabeth II of England traces her genealogy and Great Britain traces its proud heritage. In 1066 intruders entered England under William the Conqueror of Normandy who, rather than enslave the English, gradually mingled with them and strengthened the monarchy so that it has lasted from that time to ours. William and his successors subdued Ireland in 1172, Wales in 1284, and Scotland in 1296. While not permanent, this rule left a legacy of parliamentary institutions, civil rights for subjects, and a centralized state which provided the basis for a unitary culture. As on the Continent, religious strife was no stranger and a certain sense of nationalistic rivalry and separate tradition has persisted from that time to ours, between the British, the Scotch and the Welsh, not to mention the Irish.

The Roman, medieval, and Gothic ages of the British Isles gave rise to numerous quaint Christmas and year-end ceremonies, festivities, and religious observances.

part of the enormous outdoor bonfires kindled during the winter solstice to drive away evil spirits and their shelter of darkness, the Yule log earned its welcome during the feudal and medieval periods when hungry fireplaces consumed the logs in return for light and warmth. The Yule log was dragged to the household, festooned with ribbons, in triumphal processions. The yule log procession was once a good omen to all who participated. It signaled a time to burn the hatchet, to forgive one's enemies, to patch up quarrels, and to join hands at the wassail bowl. According to ritual, the log was supposed to be kept burning through all 12 days of Christmas, then be stored inside the house so that the charred remains would protect the home from fire, lightning, and more abstract evils. The following year the embers were rekindled to light a new log. Sometimes ashes from the

Scotland

While the Saturnalia, a Roman festival of fire and light coupled to wild celebrations, took place in the south, the pre-Christian festivities of the Yule, with its many lights, evergreens, and fires blazed through the frosty air of the north. The year-end ceremonies, however, were not entirely alien south from north. Norsemen, Celts, and Teutons were not so different from Roman predecessors. Thus the Church prudently decided rather than attempt to suppress established customs, to blend new meanings and holy rituals with the old Saturnalia and the Yule.

Derived from Scandinavian invaders in the 11th century, the Yule log survives from pagan antiquity. Once

Yule log were mixed with seeds in the spring so as to guarantee a good crop in the fall. In Cornwall the Yule log was known as the Mock, explaining why children were permitted to remain up until midnight on Christmas Eve to "drink to the Mock." Because today's fireplaces are in miniature by comparison, the log survives more in the shape of cakes and decorations than as actual timbers.

At Dunster in Somerset and in Devon the custom has evolved into distinctly new traditions. The head of the household cuts nine brands of green ash to form a faggot, which is lighted with fragments from last year's torch.

54

Ash, it seems, has been associated with witchcraft and divination since time immemorial. Legend reminds us that Saxon warriors in Wessex about the year 878 won many winter battles because of their discovery that ash would burn even when green; thus the soldiers could warm themselves before engaging the enemy. Traditionally, young unmarried women were each allowed to select an ash sprig; the woman whose brand first spit a spark would be the first to marry. At modern-day parties, when a sap-filled ash torch spits off a spark, it occasions nothing more than a fresh round of cider.

From community to community in the rural areas of England and Scotland the customs and traditions vary almost endlessly. While some have died out only to be revived again, others continue as they were practiced centuries ago. At Salisbury and in a few other cities, a

hum Psalm 100 on Christmas Eve, while cattle allegedly turn toward the east at midnight on December 25 and bow seven times according to the ancient system of numerical folklore.

In the home, bread baked on Christmas Eve is considered to have medicinal value for whatever ails you. In the mining areas, people formerly claimed to hear invisible choristers singing a high mass deep in the earth, while in the homes families gathered to feast on boar's head, a favorite tradition probably adopted from the invading Scandinavians. It was arranged on a silver platter with an apple in its mouth and bathed in holly, mistletoe, and rosemary. The culinary boar was outlawed during the Puritan Commonwealth but later revived in some areas. One notable place is Queen's College, Oxford, where the boar's head is served in a procession of waiters

Wales

boy from the cathedral choir is chosen bishop on St. Nicholas Day, December 6, and he reigns until Holy Innocents Day, December 28. During this time he performs all the duties and enjoys the privileges of a real bishop. Festivities include a parade, a dinner, and a sermon by the young bishop. The famous Cathedral at Salisbury houses an effigy in full vestment of such a boy bishop who died during his playful reign. On Christmas Eve the sextons at Dewsbury in Yorkshire ring the Devil's Knell. The knell consists of one toll for each year since the birth of Christ, to commemorate his triumph over the devil. Beekeepers still claim that their charges

led by trumpeters and a choir. Roasted fowl have taken the place of the boar's head in many families today; turkey, geese, capons, or pheasants now grace the tray of bounty. At one time peacocks were also Christmas fare, being described as "food for lovers and meat for lords." But King James I so liked turkey that he referred to this adopted American specialty as "the king of birds and the bird of kings." In olden times, in fact, it became customary to drive live turkeys into London a few weeks before Christmas, grazing them enroute along the roadsides. Mince pies are as popular today as in times past, in part because the meat and vegetables resting on a bed of pastry crust is likened to the manger in which Christ lay. Due to objections by the Puritans, however, mincemeat pie has evolved from a main course to a dessert filled with raisins, apples, peels, almonds, and, perhaps, a little chopped meat. Plum pudding also has retained its former prominence, though it too evolved from an earlier soup into a dessert made from raisins, candied citron, chopped figs, dried bread crumbs, and flour. The mixture is cooked with fruit juice and beaten eggs, left to jell, then served with a sweet sauce. Apparently, this pudding once was the dish known as frumenty, a gruel of milk-soaked wheat kernels flavored with sugar, spice, and raisins and served first thing on Christmas Day.

Well over a thousand years old now is the English tradition of mumming at Christmastide; one that, like the turkey, has made its way to the United States, especially for the Thanksgiving season. Dressed in costume and paper masks as different characters from history, mummers enact ancient rituals, mimic Oliver Cromwell, imitate Nelson or Napoleon, or, perhaps, characterize St. George doing battle with Beelzebub. In Hampshire whole plays are enacted by mummers, sometimes with grotesque faces of papier-mâché or wood. In a few communities the mummers are replaced with pantomime, which is patterned on a long list of fairy tales. Among them are "Cinderella," "Mother Goose," and "Robinson Crusoe." In London, this art has especially come to light in the Peter Pan story, which began in 1904 and has continued strong until this day. Norwich Theater, among others, stages elaborate pantomime productions, such as "Jack and the Beanstalk," "Puss in Boots," and "Aladdin." In Lincoln, along with the annual Christmas Fair, the "Nativity Play" is done in the mummer tradition of mockery and comic.

Of course no British Christmas would be authentic without hundreds of Christmas carols. Carols seem to have originated in France where the *carole* was originally a special circle dance accompanied with song. But they found resonance in a British tradition of pagan ring dances, which were performed especially at Stonehenge. From 1521 to the present the treasury of English carols has grown steadily. Many originally were written in English; others crossed the channel from the continent and were translated into English. "O Come, All Ye Faithful," "O Little Town of Bethlehem," and "It Came upon a Midnight Clear" are all familiar to British subjects.

In many districts of England the carolers are called "waits," a word that seems to come from the "watchmen" of former centuries, who used to join together at Christmastime, singing at various households while making their rounds. Led by a "shouter," the waits carried musical instruments and often collected funds to be used for a party on Twelfth Night. Other carolers are more solemn, such as the world famous group from King's College, Cambridge, who broadcast to the world while singing by candlelight. Numerous prominent churches, among them York Minster and King's College Chapel, Cambridge, put on a carol service, usually the Nine Lessons and Carols.

In England there is neither Santa Claus nor the Christkindlein of German tradition. Rather, Father Christmas is the one who brings toys and stuffs children's stockings. A popular custom for young children, in addition to mailing letters to Father Christmas, is to write a list of desired items and throw it into the hearth. If the paper is sucked up the chimney, the writer will get the toys. But if it burns, the child either must write another list or worry that he or she does not deserve any rewards this year.

In Ireland a candle is placed in the front window of one's home to illumine the way for the holy family. On Christmas Eve, as the family gathers to commemorate the Savior's birth, the youngest child (preferably a young girl named Mary) stands at the hearth holding a small branch of pine. At the moment when the Angelus bell rings, she takes a flame from the hearth and carries it to the candle.

Following Christmas Day with the usual mass and family celebrations, Irish revelry heats up for the feast of St. Stephen, December 26, with the Wren Boys' march. Young men of the parish first hunt down a wren and then attach the dead bird to a holly bush and march from house to house singing the following wren song at each:

> The wren, the wren, the king of all birds
> St. Stephen's day was caught in the furze;
> Although he is little, his family is great,
> So rise up, landlady, and give us a treat;
> Bottles of whiskey and bottles of beer,
> And I wish you all a happy New Year.

The tradition of the wren hunt reaches far back in the Irish past to a time when the Danes had invaded but were found sleeping by the Irish. Their drummer boy had finished eating and dozed off, when a wren spotted crumbs on the drum head and alighted to peck them up. Alarmed, the boy woke up, spotted the Irish, and began pounding his drum to awaken the Danes, who in turn not only defended themselves but attacked and defeated the Irish troops. Thus young Irishmen today hunt down a wren on Christmas Day, if possible, for the Wren Boys' march on December 26.

As in many other lands, Christmas Eve in some Irish homes is also the time for young girls to learn the identity of their future husband. According to one tradition, a maiden who sets a bowl of water outside a window to freeze will learn her future husband's identity from the form the ice takes. Another tradition calls on young women to place an onion in each of four corners of the living room; each onion is painted with the name of a man whom she would like to marry. The first onion to send forth a green shoot before January 6 identifies her future husband.

In Ireland the 12 days of Christmas end on January 6, known as "Small Christmas" or as "Women's Christmas," the day on which holly is removed from the home and burned in the hearth. Leaving decorations up beyond Twelfth Night is thought to bring bad luck in the new year. Then 12 candles are lighted from the hearth, one in honor of each of the 12 apostles. Each is lit, if possible, by a separate member of the family. The candles are then left to burn into the night.

In several Irish areas the eve of January 6 used to be associated with the wedding feast of Cana as alluded to in the rhyme that follows:

Ireland

On the night of the Three Kings
Water becomes wine,
Clusters of rushes become silk,
And the sand becomes gold.

This tradition continues in some Irish-American households where children wait up, not on January 6, but on New Year's Eve in hopes of witnessing the changing of water into wine.

Back on the English mainland, St. Stephen's Day once saw horse ceremonies, races, and packs of foxhounds matched with elegant riders on their steeds. The many ribbons and decorations now mask an ancient bleeding ceremony, which, it was believed, brought the horse good health. Perhaps this custom derived from a pagan practice of periodically sacrificing a horse to the gods. At any rate, December 26 is now known not as St. Stephen's Day so much as Boxing Day. The name refers to the alms boxes from the churches and streets that were opened only on the day after Christmas and their contents distributed to the needy. Like modern clay piggy banks, the alms boxes often had to be broken in order to release their cache. The custom of giving to the less fortunate grew over the centuries to include gifts from employers and managers to policemen, postmen, caretakers, newspaper boys, and other community servants. The modern practice is for firms to give their employees a Christmas bonus.

New Year's Day is a major event in Scotland where "first footing" is highly ritualized. The first person, or "first footer," to enter a house uninvited on New Year's Day generally brings symbolic gifts of bread, salt, a piece of coal, a few coins, and a sprig of evergreen. The devices insure good luck and happiness throughout the year. Such a visitor is supposed to be a man, have dark hair, have no physical defects, and be a stranger. For a female to enter the house first on New Year's Day is to let in bad luck during the forthcoming year.

In Presbyterian Scotland it is thought best to begin the day the way you want the year itself to go: rise early, pay your debts and borrow no more, have plenty of money in your pocket, dine well, be cheerful, and determine to work hard. Generosity and good wishes often extend to extra portions for the animals in the Highlands.

All over England New Year celebrations include the ubiquitous wassail bowl, a word that derives from the Saxon phrase of *waes hael*, meaning "to be in good health" and "to be fortunate." The custom of wassailing seems to have arisen with the Danes when they briefly ruled England. Sometimes on New Year's Eve or on the Eve of Epiphany, farmers wassail their apple trees by drinking toasts of cider and shooting guns into the bare branches. This is done to assure a good harvest. At Wick in northern Scotland the old year is actually burned out with great bonfires, around which the people dance with lighted torches before partaking from the wassail bowl. At Stonehaven paraffin-soaked rope balls bagged in wire netting are torched into flaming firebrands, then swung round at the end of a cord. This tradition is accompanied by farmers firing their guns to shoot the old year out and the new one in, all of which is followed by the traditional wassail.

In Herfordshire and other West Country communities, the farmers gather on Twelfth Night to eat hot cakes soaked in cider. While neighbors assemble to bang on pots and shoot into the apple trees, the guests joyfully sing the wassail songs and drink cider. In the Norfolk, Wiltshire, Carhampton, and Somerset rural districts, similar wassailing parties, sometimes called "apple-howling," fill the night air, seemingly to purify the orchards and fields for better vegetation and harvests the next summer. In the north, wassailers carry wooden bowls on their heads from house to house, singing old rhymes or traditional carols.

Related to the aforementioned swinging of fireballs is the custom at Burghead, Morayshire, of "burning the clavie." The clavie is a half-barrel filled with tar and carried on a pole. The pitch is lighted with a firebrand (never a match) and carried round the town in a procession led by the Clavie King. It ends on a hill outfitted with a Roman altar on which the burning barrel is posted, to be hacked to bits by the king and his men while crowds gather to garner a burning ember as a good luck charm. This charm must then be mounted on one's chimney to ward off witches and evil spirits.

Similarly at Allendale in Northumberland, young men march through town carrying barrels of burning tar on their heads. They end up at a heap of wood on which all the bearers toss their blazing tubs to create a gigantic bonfire. The crowds then dance and revel around the bonfire until daybreak. In early morning many of these fire bearers become "first footers" for the community. In a few communities in South Wales young men draw fresh spring water and process from house to house blessing and sprinkling everything in sight for a prosperous new year, including those still in bed when possible. Always welcome are a few pennies to support a party later that evening. At St. Ives in Cornwall young men blacken their faces for a street dance held on the first fortnight of the new year when they also enter houses to leave kisses and blackened faces, it being an ill omen for a house to have been overlooked.

After New Year's Day and Epiphany farmers turn their thoughts to spring ploughing. More specifically all workers think of going back to their jobs following the year-end festivities. Thus the first Sunday following January 6 is Plough Sunday, which gives farmers an opportunity to bring their implements to church to be blessed; meanwhile the remainder of the work force only symbolically "takes up the plough" the following Monday. The plough ceremonies are especially noteworthy in Exeter and Chichester Cathedrals.

Closely associated with Plough Sunday is Epiphany or, in the British tradition, Twelfth Night. At St. James Palace a special service is held in which frankincense, myrrh, and gold are offered to the Christ child. The gifts are then passed on to institutions for common uses. Twelfth Night cakes show up in most homes. In a few communities the people elect a Twelfth Day king, identified as the one who discovers a pea in his piece of cake. Already the plays, masked balls, and revelry point to the pre-Lenten season. Indeed, by Twelfth Night, the Christmas season is rapidly fading.

Christmas Corners

The Christmas Eve Service

GRAHAM HUNTER

The Christmas Charm

PAT CORRICK HINTON

Two weeks left until Christmas! Snow was falling at last, and Hattie felt better than she had for a long time. She pushed a gray strand of hair back from her eyes, turned the blackened rag to a clean spot, and dipped it into the silver polish.

"Nutmeg," she said to the calico curled up by the heat vent, "did you ever see such a bracelet? Just look at all these charms. Ginny will love it. I think it's the perfect Christmas gift for her. Don't you?" Hattie jangled the bracelet at the cat who looked sleepily at her then curled up again.

Hattie had bought the bracelet for a few dollars a week ago at a flea market, but this was the first chance she'd really had to examine it. The heart charm had caught her eye first that day, the light reflecting its silver at just the right angle. She knew her only niece Ginny would treasure it along with the many other charms she collected.

"Dear Ginny," she thought, "all that time she spent with me last winter after Pete died. I'd never have made it without her."

Hattie held up the bracelet at arms length. Shining it up made her feel she was personalizing it a little. She turned the small table lamp brighter, picked up a magnifying glass, and settled in for a closer look. She grinned and shook her head.

"Cat, I'm sure of it. This bracelet tells a story. Now, come over here and listen. It will give you sweet dreams for sure." Hattie bent over and put the cat on her lap. Within seconds, Nutmeg was purring contentedly.

"You see, love, this is the story of R. C. who fell in love with J. O. and gave her a bracelet with this silver heart charm and their initials. The palm tree says 1970, so that's probably when they got married and went to

Hawaii for their honeymoon. And this must be their house. Look at it, Nutmeg. Three-dimensional and even a chimney. Now this ballerina and diver must mean they love ballet and swimming, or else they have kids who do. Here are golf clubs and skis. Such active people! And look at these dogs! Do you suppose they really *own* that many dogs?"

Nutmeg stretched out a leg and let it dangle, content with the drone of Hattie's voice, just so long as she could stay on her lap.

Hattie giggled. "Cat. This is such fun! I should have been a detective. Oh, what's this? A little trophy. And there's a name: C-A-R-L-I-N and . . . oh, oh, the year 1984 on the back." Hattie clasped the bracelet to her chest. A different feeling came over her. The anonymous R. C. suddenly became R. Carlin, a real person.

Hattie looked at the bracelet in her hand. "If this really does tell a story then someone must be missing it. But if R. Carlin gave it to J. O., how could she ever part with it? Kitty, 1984 was just last year! What could have happened?"

Nutmeg had to jump down as Hattie suddenly got up from her chair and walked into the living room. Twilight was casting blue shadows over the mounds of snow outside. Inside, the undecorated room seemed more bare than ever as a heaviness settled over Hattie. The joy of the bracelet's story was gone. She slumped into an overstuffed chair, staring out at the snow and then down at the bracelet. Singling out the heart, she gave in to the memories of her own falling in love with Pete. There had never been anyone but Pete. For 30 years they had never missed a Christmas together; now he was gone.

"Much too soon," she thought. "How can I even think of this Christmas without him?" She opened and closed

60

the clasp. "If these charms were to tell our story," she said half aloud, "I would start with a heart, too, and there would have to be an old Buick for all the trips we took together . . . and a fish for all the trout Pete caught and I cooked . . . and roses, lots of roses, for all the years of pleasure we got from growing them. . . ."

Hattie sat without moving, overwhelmed by memories and loneliness. She was holding the bracelet so tightly the pain of it digging into her palm brought her back to the darkening living room. She sighed and looked at the groove in her hand. "This bracelet's the most fun I've had in ages," she thought. "So much for that. I can hardly send it to Ginny for a present if it belongs to someone else. Guess I'd better find out who."

As if that were too much, the tears came pouring out, and Hattie let go of the pain she so carefully kept hidden from others. Many minutes later, she made her way to the bathroom and splashed cold water on her face. Nutmeg rubbed comfortingly against her legs. Hattie picked her up and held her close to her face as she walked to the bedroom. "What will become of me, cat? Good thing I have you," she said, setting her down on the soft quilt. "At least you need me."

Hattie recovered her normal reserve the next day and purposely ignored the bracelet over the weekend, leaving it buried in the folds of the chair. On Monday, her longtime friend, Gwen, stopped to pick her up for their weekly quilting party, and Hattie impulsively grabbed it on her way out the door. "Bet the girls have never seen anything quite like this," she said to herself, dropping it into her pocket. "Anyhow, R. Carlin could live anywhere in this country. Right now, it's mine." Hattie climbed into the car and shook the charms at Gwen. "Have I got a story for you, Gwen!"

"You sure look good for a person who might have to push this car if we get stuck in the snow," Gwen teased. "Don't tell me that's the bracelet you bought for your niece at the flea market?"

"Yes, it is, and these charms tell a story. It's fascinating! Wait till you hear!"

Over lunch, Hattie told her charm story to the other women, enjoying their reactions. She left out the assumptions she had made of the name and year.

"I thought I'd give it to my niece Ginny, you know, the one from Arizona that stayed with me last winter," she concluded, hoping she wouldn't have to say more.

Several of them nodded and went on to discuss their children and grandchildren, and who was getting what for Christmas. Hattie sat there, trying as always to be interested in their families but feeling quite alone and more aware than ever of the differences in their lives. It grew to a gnawing feeling until she couldn't wait to get home, even though she knew what awaited her there.

The minute she got in the door, she went to the phone book. There was a long column of Carlins, five with the initial R. Hattie sighed. "Should I or shouldn't I, cat? What do you think the odds are that one of these Carlins is missing this bracelet? Pretty good, you say? Yes, I'm afraid so. Can you tell me why all this has to happen now? Isn't Christmas tough enough this year?"

Hattie squared her shoulders and began to copy down the R. Carlins and their numbers. The first lived on Ingersoll. Hattie swallowed as she considered what she would say. She dialed, letting it ring 10 times. No an-

swer. The next two lived on University and both sounded like students. They knew nothing about a charm bracelet and left her feeling a little foolish for asking. The fourth Carlin lived on 42nd street, but there was no answer there, either.

"One more to try," she muttered as she dialed the last number on Grand Avenue. A woman answered on the first ring. Surprised, Hattie blurted out, "Oh, I'm sorry to bother you, but could you tell me if anyone at this number has lost a charm bracelet?"

The voice on the other end cackled. "Bracelet? What kind did you say? Charms? Sure. I lost a charm bracelet. Real expensive, too. Why don't you describe it to me?"

Hattie opened her mouth ready to oblige then thought better of it. Warily she asked, "Perhaps you could tell *me* what the bracelet looks like."

"Oh, so that's the way is it! Well, mine has lots of expensive stones set in the charms, one for each of my husbands." The voice cackled again.

Hattie signed off politely, realizing how careful she would have to be. "I wonder if all this is necessary," she thought. "Maybe I should just enjoy it for a while and send it on to Ginny. I'm probably making too much out of all this."

For the next few days, Hattie did enjoy it. She had a great time showing it to the children she visited on her volunteer day at the hospital. Over and over she told her story to the children and nurses, spicing it up just a little each time. The more she talked about it, the more attached to the bracelet she became. Maybe she should even keep it for herself! But, by Wednesday, Hattie knew she'd better at least try calling the numbers again. At suppertime, she tried the 42nd Street number. A man with a deep voice answered.

"Uh-um. Hello. Is this the Carlin residence?"

"Yes, it is."

"I, uh, have come into possession of a charm bracelet and there is an R. Carlin engraved on it. I wonder if it might belong to someone in your house."

"Yes, as a matter of fact, we are missing a bracelet. What are the charms like?"

"Well, uh, if you don't mind, I'd like you to describe them to me." Hattie took a deep breath.

The man described the bracelet exactly. Hattie agreed it must be theirs and offered to bring it to their home.

There was a pause.

"I'm sorry. I just can hardly believe this. Who is this calling, anyhow?"

"My name is Hattie Franklin, Mr. Carlin. I live over near the parkway. I bought the bracelet as a gift for my niece at a flea market. It's beautiful and the charms seem to tell a story. . . ."

"Ahem, yes," broke in Mr. Carlin. "My wife's bracelet is beautiful, and it does tell a story. Uh, listen. Are you sure you don't mind dropping it off?"

Hattie assured him and agreed to come around seven that evening. She arrived one minute before the hour, curious at her own need to know the people behind the charms. A young girl around 10 years old answered the door.

"May I see Mr. Carlin, please? I'm Mrs. Franklin. He's expecting me."

"Sure, c'mon in. Are you the one who found my mom's bracelet?"

"Yes, I am. Or maybe it found me," Hattie answered with a small laugh.

A tall couple appeared in the doorway. "Handsome pair," Hattie thought, "probably in their mid-thirties." Both were smiling and looked questioningly at Hattie as they shook hands.

"We're Jan and Richard Carlin, Mrs. Franklin. Please come in and sit down."

Hattie sat down on the sofa and the others grouped themselves around her. A small boy joined them, and both children grinned intently at Hattie. Hattie smiled back, noticing their big blue eyes and healthy good looks.

"Uh, ma'am. Could we see the bracelet?"

"Oh, yes. I was admiring your children. Here it is."

"That's it! That's really it," shrieked Jan as she took it from Hattie's hand. "Incredible! I'm so glad to see this again." The girl put her arm around her mother's shoulders.

"Where exactly did you find it again, Mrs. Franklin? On the phone you said something about a flea market." Jan and Richard exchanged glances.

Hattie described how she came upon the bracelet, leaving out the interpretation she had given the charms.

Richard shook his head. "This is really something. Believe it or not, this bracelet was stolen from us last year. We were out of town for my mother's funeral when our home here was broken into. They took our TV and stereo, even wrapped Christmas gifts, and lots of little stuff. The appliances were marked with identification, but the pre-

sents and things like this were impossible to replace. I guess you can see how much your returning this means to my wife. By the way, these are our children, Lisa and Joe."

Both children continued grinning at Hattie, making her feel wonderfully at ease.

Lisa said, "My mom says the bracelet is a keepsake and a treasure 'cuz it tells the story of our family."

"Yes, I thought it might. I've been imagining all sorts of things."

"Really? Like what?" Joe asked, sitting down near Hattie's feet.

The family all looked expectantly at Hattie, so she started in with how they might have met and told her version right up to 1984. "I felt so bad when I saw the year because it's so recent. It's such a unique idea, the way it tells a story. I've had a lot of fun telling friends what I imagined . . . oh." Hattie stopped, shocked that she'd given away her affection for it.

Mrs. Carlin smiled. "You were mostly right about the meaning of the charms, except that we honeymooned in Nassau, not Hawaii. We do love sports, and that trophy is a miniature of one that our youngest dog won at a big show last year. We raise cockers for show, and for fun, I guess." They all laughed. Mrs. Carlin put a hand on Hattie's arm. "You know, Mrs. Franklin, we're so lucky someone as honest as you found the bracelet."

"Right! And it seems to me that a reward is in order," said Mr. Carlin.

They all agreed excitedly, but Hattie declined and made motions to leave.

Mrs. Carlin stood up. "Please, Mrs. Franklin, at least stay and have some coffee and cake with us. I can't tell you how grateful I am to have these charms back, and I'd like to do something for you. Won't you stay with us a little while?"

Hattie agreed, feeling content and drawn toward this warm family.

As Mrs. Carlin disappeared with the children, Hattie turned to Mr. Carlin, "I'm glad I could get this back to you, especially after all the problems you've had lately."

"Problems and heartache. That's for sure. In two years Jan and I both lost our parents. Then all these other things." He shook his head. "Makes a person wonder. The worst of it is the kids suddenly have no grandparents. They feel a big hole in their lives now, an emptiness."

Something stirred in Hattie. "Yes, I know what you mean. I lost my husband almost a year ago. I'm still trying to fill that gap."

Suddenly, with clatter and giggles, the polished table was filled with chocolate Bundt cake, coffee, and milk. Hattie ate and chatted with the family for nearly a half hour. The conversation flowed easily; by the time she felt she must go they were on a first-name basis. As she walked to the door, they hovered around her, shaking her hand and urging her to come back for another visit.

"We won't ever forget you, Hattie. We want you to come back," Jan said.

"I'd like that," Hattie said. "You have a beautiful family, and I hope things will start looking up for you now."

She drove off with a wave, looking back at the group in the doorway. "I'll never forget you either," she thought.

And she didn't forget them. Every child she saw the next day during her Christmas shopping reminded her of the Carlin children. First thing that morning she had carefully selected a new charm for Ginny's collection. It was attractive but not nearly as interesting as Jan Carlin's bracelet. Now she was trying to find some small gifts for her quilter friends, but instead found herself wandering over to the toys and children's clothing.

By noon a fresh snowfall had made shopping hazardous. Hattie was glad she had taken the bus downtown instead of trying to fight traffic and snow in a car. As the clock on the top of the old bank struck the hour, Hattie and Gwen ordered lunch at their usual meeting place. During their soup and sandwich Hattie told Gwen what had happened to the bracelet. Gwen was amazed.

"You probably did the right thing, Hattie, but I'm surprised you could give it up. You really wanted your niece to have it."

"Yes, I did. But if you could have seen the look on Jan's face, well, it was worth it all. Anyway, it would always bother me, wondering whose it was. I bought a nice new charm for Ginny; she'll never know the difference. Now I think maybe I'll get the children something."

"Now don't get carried away, Hattie. You only saw them once."

"I know, Gwen, but there was something about them."

Gwen studied her friend a moment. "Well, why don't you give them a call. It can't hurt."

Hattie brightened. "Do you really think so? Do I dare invite them over? Gwen, I'd love to have them come to my home. I haven't forgotten how to make cookies. And maybe I could get a little tree. Would they come, do you think?"

"Of course they would. Now let's get a move on or we'll miss our bus."

When they emerged from the restaurant, the bus was almost to the corner. Grappling with shopping bags and gloves and purses, they rushed to the opening doors. Gwen got on, but as Hattie started to step up, her foot slipped on a small patch of packed snow. Her knee went down with a crack as it hit the icy sidewalk. She groaned and fell to her side, vaguely hearing someone ask if she was hurt. She thought she saw Gwen reach down to her. Then, everything went black.

When she awoke later, Gwen was saying, "Hattie, you gave me the scare of my life." There were other words too, something about a broken leg and plastic screw, then she floated away to sleep again.

For the next few days, Hattie was aware only of pain and a need to sleep, and a glimpse of Gwen every so

often. At the end of the week she was well enough to sit up in bed and listen to a group of carolers. Her roommate informed her that Christmas was only one week away. They both groaned to think they might spend it in the hospital.

As the carolers moved down the hall, Gwen appeared in the doorway, grinning from ear to ear.

"Hi, Hattie! How's it going? My, my, don't you look nice today? Hair all brushed and even some color in your face. I just stopped by your house to pick up a few things you might be needing. I even found a can of your favorite Spanish peanuts. I hear they work wonders for broken legs."

They both laughed. Hattie gave Gwen a big hug. "You're a lifesaver, Gwen. It's wonderful to be feeling alive again."

"Well, I told you before and I'll tell you again, Hattie Franklin, you gave me the scare of my life." Gwen paused, "It's good you're sort of fancied up today because I have another surprise for you. As I was coming out of your house a little group of people was just about to ring your doorbell. When I found out who they were, I decided they just might be the best medicine you could get in this place. The nurse is going to take you down the hall to the lounge so you can see them."

Gwen settled Hattie in her wheelchair near a window in the lounge. She stepped back and intoned, "Ta-daa!"

Hattie's mouth flew open as the Carlins filed in. Hattie couldn't find words, but she smiled in amazement.

"We went to your house to bring you a little Christmas gift, Hattie. Your friend Gwen convinced us to bring it here to the hospital. How are you feeling?" Jan asked.

"Better, thanks," said Hattie as Lisa put a small box into her hands.

"Merry Christmas, Hattie," she said beaming. "Aren't you going to open it?"

Hattie looked at Lisa, then at the package. Finally she started to open it. The wrapping was bright green with thank-yous printed all over it. She pulled off the red bow and carefully unfolded the white tissue inside. Lying on smooth white cotton was a shiny silver charm bracelet.

Hattie gasped, looking around at the family and then at Gwen. Her eyes filled as she examined each charm. In the center was a large silver Christmas tree with a small pearl near the top. Next to the tree were a ballerina and a diver. On the other side was a round disc engraved with R. C. + J. C. ♡ H.F.

Hattie struggled to say, "It's beautiful. Thank you."

Joe moved in closer and said, "Hattie, there's more. Turn the Christmas tree over." Hattie searched Joe's eyes, then turned the charm over. Engraved in tiny letters were the words: "To Grandma."